The Development
of Underdevelopment
in China

The Development
of Underdevelopment
in China

A SYMPOSIUM

Edited by Philip C. C. Huang

M.E. SHARPE, INC.,
WHITE PLAINS, NEW YORK

Originally published in *Modern China*, Vol. 4, No. 3
(July 1978), and Vol. 6, No. 1 (January 1980).
This edition published in 1980 by M. E. Sharpe, Inc.,
901 North Broadway, White Plains, New York 10603
by arrangement with Sage Publications, Inc.

Library of Congress Catalog Card Number: 80-51203
International Standard Book Number: 0-87332-164-2

Printed in the United States of America

Contents

The Development of Underdevelopment in China

VICTOR D. LIPPIT

University of California, Riverside

*The history of China has shown no
development, so that we cannot concern
ourselves with it any further.*

—Hegel

INTRODUCTION

During the Song Dynasty (960-1279), an economic revolution
swept over China. The development of wet-field rice cultivation
in conjunction with a great southward migration led to sharply
higher land productivity in agriculture. At the same time, rapid
expansion in domestic and foreign trade accompanied urban
growth, and for certain commodities the market became a
national one. The growing commercialization of the economy led
to increasing sophistication in the means of exchange, and by the
end of the eleventh century paper money was used in much of

AUTHOR'S NOTE: *I am indebted for critical comments on a preliminary draft of this
essay to Joseph Esherick especially and also to Jerome Chen, Linda Grove, Philip Huang,
James Parsons, and Irwin Wall, all of whom, however, I absolve of responsibility for
the results. This essay constitutes the first section of my forthcoming book,* The Economic
Development of China, *to be published by M. E. Sharpe, Inc.*

China (Elvin, 1973: 159). The entire Song period was marked by technological and organizational innovation, with the transmission of new ideas and techniques facilitated by the spread of woodblock printing, which came into general use early in the period (Elvin, 1973: 179; Balazs, 1972: 42).

The principal features of the agricultural revolution included improved soil preparation based on new knowledge, tools and fertilizers, new seed strains that increased yields or made two crops possible by ripening earlier, the extension and improvement of irrigation and hydraulic techniques generally, and the increased specialization in production, including the development of crops other than foodgrains, that the growing commercialization of the economy made possible. The practical agricultural treatises which appeared with the spread of printing were read by the educated landowners and contributed to the dissemination of the improved techniques. By the thirteenth century, Chinese agriculture was among the most sophisticated and productive in the world.

In foreign trade, Song China exported a wide range of goods, including textiles, porcelain, tea, precious metals, lead and tin, while importing incense, perfumes, spices, pearls, ivory, coral, amber, shells, agates, crystal, and other luxury goods (Balazs, 1972: 63). Trade reached from Japan in the east to South Asia, the Near East, and Africa in the west. During the Tang Dynasty (618-906), domestic shipping was already extensively developed; in the eighth century, the Commissioner for Salt and Iron had ordered 2,000 boats built for service on the Yangzi (Yangtze) with a capacity equal to one-third that of Britain's merchant fleet in the eighteenth century (Elvin, 1973: 136). During the Song dynasty, improvements in ship technology made Chinese ships preeminent in foreign trade as well (Elvin, 1973: 137), and the further development of river and canal shipping played a major role in the development of the national market.

By Song times the towns had become thoroughly urban in character, with merchants and artisans constituting the majority of the inhabitants. More striking, however, was the development of large cities and a sophisticated civilization of great complexity and specialization. The most developed city of all was Hangzhou (Hangchow), the capital from 1135 of the Southern Song (1127-1279), a city of which we have extensive, detailed accounts by a number of contemporary observers.

In 1270, on the eve of the Mongol invasion, the population of Hangzhou exceeded one million (Gernet, 1970: 38, 84). The two dozen trades included masons, carpenters, potters, brick-makers, weavers, tailors, gilders, lacquer workers, and makers of oil and candles (Balazs, 1972: 90). Merchants specializing in luxury goods and the necessities of life were numerous and flourishing. A contemporary account of the city's tea-houses explains,

> They make arrangements of the flowers of the four seasons, hang up paintings by celebrated artists, decorate the walls of the estab-lishment, and all the year round sell unusual teas and curious soups. During the winter months, they sell in addition a very fine powdered tea, pancakes, onion tea, and sometimes soup of salted beans. During the hot season they add as extras plum-flower wine with a mousse of snow, a beverage for contracting the gall-bladder, and herbs against the heat, etc. . . . At present, the tea-houses lay out a display of flowers, in which are arranged curious pines, strange cypresses, and other plants. The walls of the room are decorated, and business is done to the click of clappers and the sound of singing. Only porcelain cups are used, and things are served on lacquer trays [Balazs, 1972: 94].[1]

While the tea-houses typically served as rendezvous points for off-duty officials and young men of wealthy families, there were also tea-houses that served especially as meeting places for laborers, domestic servants, and artisans of the various crafts. For those more concerned with eating than with meeting, the city's elegant restaurants offered a wide range of choice, including restaurants for noodles and jiaozi, vegetarian restaurants, patisseries, inns and bars, pubs, low-class eating houses, and restaurants offering a choice among literally hundreds of elaborate Chinese dishes. At the end of the thirteenth century, in the words of Gernet (1970: 18), "In the spheres of social life, art, amusements, institutions and technology, China was incontestably the most advanced country of the time."

The contrast with the first half of the twentieth century could not be more striking. Some six and a half centuries later, China was among the poorest, most underdeveloped countries in the world. In 1933, the entire modern sector accounted for some 7% of gross domestic product (GDP), with per capita product coming to slightly over U.S. $60 (Perkins, 1975: 119, 125). Even this low per capita income figure can be highly misleading as an index of welfare, however, for it fails to take into account the gross inequalities in the distribution of income, the systematic exploitation of labor in the countryside and cities, unemployment, underemployment, and corrupt, ineffective government. All of these characteristic features of underdevelopment marked Chinese life in the century preceding the success of China's socialist revolution in 1949. In this study, I am concerned primarily with analyzing the process by which China, the world's most advanced country in 1270, became one of the world's most underdeveloped countries by 1949. In other words, I am concerned with the process of the development of underdevelopment in China.

To explore this process, I shall turn in the next section to a summary sketch of some principal features of China's economic history. This sketch is admittedly most cursory; its purpose is principally to provide a backdrop for the ensuing discussion of theories of underdevelopment. These theories fit into two main categories: some of them are major theses in the literature of economic development that attempt to explain the phenomenon of underdevelopment, while the others have been articulated by China-specialists—historians, economists, and others—seeking to explain the Chinese experience specifically. While the categories are not always clearly distinguished (China-specialists have of course often made use of more general theories), I have found it convenient to distinguish three of the more general arguments from three of those developed in a specifically Chinese context.

While some of the theories provide important insights, none of them is adequate to account for the development of underdevelopment in China. I go on, accordingly, to provide my own account, focusing on the class structure and use of the economic surplus in "traditional" Chinese society, and analyzing the role of Western expansion and imperialism as a contributory but distinctly secondary factor.

A THUMBNAIL SKETCH OF CHINESE ECONOMIC HISTORY SINCE 960

During the late Tang (618-906) and Song (960-1279) dynasties, and into the early part of the subsequent period of Mongol rule (the Yuan Dynasty, 1279-1367), the Chinese economy expanded rapidly in what Elvin has termed China's "medieval economic revolution." I have already touched upon some of the agricultural, commercial, and demographic changes, including urbanization, that characterized this period. With the active encouragement and sponsorship of the state, this period was also marked by great advances in science and technology. Elvin (1973: 179) provides the following summary.

> From the tenth to the fourteenth century China advanced to the threshold of a systematic experimental investigation of nature, and created the world's earliest mechanized industry. A few examples will illustrate the range of these achievements. In mathematics, a general technique was found for the solution of numerical equations containing any power of a single unknown. In astronomy, a new level of observational accuracy was achieved with the casting of much larger instruments and the perfection of hydraulic clockwork. In medicine, a start was made upon systematic anatomy with the dissection of cadavers; more precision was attained in the description of diseases; and a vast number of new remedies [was] added to the pharmacopoeia. In metallurgy, coal certainly (and coke possibly) was used for the extraction of iron from iron ore. In warfare, gunpowder changed from a material for fireworks into a true explosive; and flame-throwers, poison gas, fragmentation bombs and the gun were invented. At the same time

there was an increasing tendency to try to relate existing theoretical systems more closely with the mass of empirical information collected in the preceding centuries, most notably in pharmacology and chemistry.

In the fourteenth century, this rapid economic and scientific progress ceased for reasons which are not entirely clear. We do know, however, that continued technological progress did not require scientific knowledge beyond Chinese attainments of the time. The reason for the end of the medieval economic revolution, therefore, is to be sought in the weakening of the social, political, and economic forces which sustain invention and innovation.

Two of the factors contributing to the decline, which appears to have lasted until the beginning of the sixteenth century, were the disappearance of the frontier and the decline of foreign trade (Elvin, 1973: 204-225).[2] As I have noted, substantial migration to south China with a much greater productivity potential than the north was associated with the rapid expansion of the medieval period. As the best lands in the south filled up, the stimulus provided by migration came to an end.

Another important stimulus was lost in the government suppression of foreign trade. While in Song and earlier times the long arm of the government had extended into commercial affairs with the licensing of trade—both a means of control and an important revenue source—increasing restrictions during the Mongol period were followed by a complete ban on foreign trade from the early Ming Dynasty (1368-1644). While the ban was partially lifted in 1567, government policy throughout the Ming and subsequent Qing (Ch'ing) Dynasty (1644-1912) was to suppress and restrict foreign trade as much as possible; although foreign trade did increase after the Opium War (1839-1842), it remained essentially peripheral to the Chinese economy throughout the imperial period.

While the possibility of encouraging licensed trade as a source of revenue was not lost upon the government, the restrictions were designed to "starve out" the pirates that flourished along the coast, prevent the smuggling of arms and the export of weapons-technology, and above all to prevent competing centers of power from being established along the coast. This latter concern was compounded by the absence of a strong imperial navy, which had been allowed to decline after the Grand Canal to Beijing was reconstructed in 1411 and the sea transport of grain eliminated in 1415. With the Yangzi basin grain necessary to sustain the capital moving north through the Grand Canal rather than along the coast, a strong navy became a luxury rather than a necessity. The restrictions on foreign trade severely damaged the economies of the principal trading centers, especially in Fujian (Fukien) province, gave rise to a flourishing smuggling industry, aided and abetted by the protection and financing of the local gentry, and foreclosed the possibility of receiving the stimulus that foreign trade sometimes affords to economic development through the transmission of new ideas and technology, invest-ment demand, and the provision of a surplus for investment through the gains of exchange.

The renewed economic expansion between the sixteenth and eighteenth centuries opened new opportunities for the propertied classes in pawn-broking, money-lending, and urban real estate as well as in the expanding domestic trade. A contemporary commentator observed:

> There are one-fold profits in agriculture and it needs very great labour. Fools do it. There are two-fold profits in manufacture and it needs great labour. Those who have skilful fingers do it. There are three-fold profits in trading, and little labour is needed. Those who are prudent and thoughtful do it. There are five-fold profits in the (illegal) sale of salt, and labour is not necessary. Bad and powerful people do it [Elvin, 1973: 248].[3]

Despite this cynical observation, income from agricultural land remained the principal source of unearned income in the country-side. In the agricultural sector of the 1930s, land rent constituted 10.7% of national income, farm business profits or the surplus produced by annually hired labor above its own consumption

3.4%, and rural interest payments 2.8% (Lippit, 1974: 76). While these percentages may well have been different in the eighteenth century, there is no reason to believe that the interest and profit income might have been higher relative to rental income at that time.

In keeping with the new sources of income, and attracted by the security as well as the amenities of urban living, by the eighteenth century most of the landlords of any substance had become urban residents. While the very largest lived in the larger cities, most lived in the provincial towns which grew up as regional market centers. "Their big, high-walled compounds enclosing many courtyards, replete with servants and hoarded supplies and proof against bandits, still dominate the old market towns" (Fairbank, 1971: 26). Their homes symbolize their role in China's economic stagnation between the late eighteenth and early twentieth centuries, for insofar as the land-owning gentry became a largely rentier class, divorced from productive activity, it is natural that innovation in the countryside languished. By comparison, the dynamic agricultural progress of early Meiji Japan and eighteenth century England rested on a resident land-holding class that was vitally concerned with improving the techniques of production.

By the eighteenth century, the class structure that characterized the first half of the twentieth century was, in the main, already established. For a population of 300-400 million, there were less than 20,000 senior government officials (Fairbank, 1971: 29-30). This was possible only because local authority was for the most part in the hands of the gentry class. Narrowly defined, this class was made up of the one and a quarter million degree holders who had passed at least the lowest level of the state examinations (Fairbank, 1971: 30), but its social and economic basis was landownership and such related activities as money-lending. Under the gentry-dominated land-owning class (3% of the agricultural population),[4] the peasants could be divided into three classes: the rich peasants (7%), middle peasants (20-30%), and poor and landless peasants (60-70%). The rich peasants, with more land than they could farm themselves, commonly hired agricultural laborers to work for them on a year-round basis. They often used the surplus generated by their farming activities to engage in trade, set up distilleries or other local enterprises, engage in money-lending, and so forth. The middle peasants typically had enough land to produce a subsistence income. The poor and landless peasants, numerically the largest group, often did not; their marginal existence during "ordinary" times left them highly vulnerable to the frequent natural and man-made calamities that wreaked havoc in the Chinese countryside and their children's chances of surviving to maturity were typically less than even. While a number of scholars have contested whether or not there was actually a decline in living standards since the middle of the nineteenth century,[5] there is no doubt about the extremity of poverty in which the majority of peasants lived in the first half of the twentieth century (Chen, 1973; Fei, 1945; Hinton, 1966; Myrdal, 1965; Yang, 1965).

The seventeenth century and most of the eighteenth was a period of thriving economic activity, but stagnation was more characteristic of the economy from the end of the eighteenth century. During the nineteenth and twentieth centuries population continued to expand slowly, but the cumulative increases were quite substantial, with the number of Chinese increasing from perhaps 275 million in 1779 to 430 million in 1850 (Ho, 1959: 64) and 500 million in 1933 (Liu and Yeh, 1965: 34-36). The major exception to the population expansion was caused by the more than 20 million deaths associated with the Taiping Revolution, the civil war which raged across much of China between 1850 and 1864.[6] During the nineteenth and first half of the twentieth centuries, moderate technological progress in Chinese agriculture made it possible for agricultural output approximately to keep pace with population growth. To some extent, the cultivation of new land also contributed, as Manchuria especially was opened to Han Chinese immigration after 1860 and in the early part of the twentieth century the migration became fairly substantial. Still, as a proportion of the total Chinese population, the number of migrants to Manchuria was quite small,[7] and for the most part China's good-quality arable land was being fully utilized long before the nineteenth century.

While the impact of the West was strongest in the nineteenth and twentieth centuries, consideration of earlier relations may help to clarify the nature of the impact. The first Europeans in the age of Western expansion to reach China were the Portuguese, who arrived at Guangzhou (Canton) in 1517. In 1519 a small Portuguese fleet which landed at Tunmen captured some slaves and bought others, concentrating on adolescent youths and girls, as had proven so profitable in Africa. Evidently reflecting a popular belief, however, the responsible Chinese officials misunderstood the routine commercial practices of the Portuguese traders, believing that they acquired children in order to eat them (see, for example, Chinese official Gu Yan-wu, quoted in Franke, 1967a: 29). From 1522 the Portuguese traders were forbidden to return to China, but as they and the merchants and officials they bribed found trade profitable, it could not be suppressed altogether. This pattern of the West achieving its purposes in non-Western countries by corrupting an elite social stratum and identifying that stratum's interest with its own would reappear in the twentieth century era of neocolonialism. In 1530 Guangzhou was reopened to foreign trade, with the Portuguese excluded but effectively permitted to trade elsewhere.

I have already noted the Ming and Qing efforts to restrict foreign trade. The government saw in it a potential threat to the political order, and given the size of China and the extent of its domestic trade, felt little need to acquire things unavailable domestically. As the Qian Long Emperor (1736-1795), responding to the English request for expanded trade relations, wrote to King George III,

> If I have commanded that the tribute offerings sent by you, O King, are to be accepted, this was solely in consideration for the spirit which prompted you to dispatch them from afar. . . . As your Ambassador can see for himself, we possess all things. I set no value on objects strange or ingenious, and have no use for your country's manufactures [Schurmann and Schell, 1967: 107-108].

The empire regarded trade as part of the tribute system, according to which nominal recognition of Chinese suzerainty by tribute-bearing emmisaries was rewarded by the emperor's permitting a limited amount of trade. The Chinese court always regarded trade as a privilege rather than as a right.

For its own part, the Chinese government proclaimed the right to a monopoly over the limited foreign trade it did permit. It did not act directly itself, however, but assigned the right to trade to a group of Chinese merchants known as the "Cohong" (*gong hang*) who exercised it as agents of the government (Franke, 1967a: 67). The foreign merchants who dealt with them, not allowed to reside in Guangzhou itself, were restricted to narrow areas outside the walls of the city. The foreigners were allowed to deal directly only with the so-called Hong merchants who, to a certain extent, were held responsible even for their behavior.

Prior to the nineteenth century the British Empire had an imbalance in its trade with China. As China exported much more than it imported, silver had to be sent to China to make up the difference. From the second half of the eighteenth century especially, English merchants discovered the profits to be made in exporting opium from British India to China, and the British actively promoted these exports to remedy the specie drain. In the nineteenth century opium exports expanded dramatically. In 1816, 3,210 chests of opium were imported into Guangzhou (each chest was about 100 catties or 110 pounds); in 1831, 16,500 chests were imported, and in 1838, 40,000 chests (Wakeman, 1966: 32). By 1829, opium changed the balance of trade and silver began flowing out of China.

Since 1729 the imperial government had banned opium smoking, and in 1800 it banned importation of the drug. Despite such efforts, however, imports increased by leaps and bounds, with renewed Chinese efforts to put a stop to them leading to the Opium War of 1839-1842. British victory was followed by the Treaty of Nanjing (Nanking) [1842], according to which the Chinese were forced to cede Hong Kong to Britain and open Guangzhou, Xiamen (Amoy), Fuzhou, Ningbo, and Shanghai to foreign trade as "treaty ports." This was the first of a series of unequal treaties that the Western powers forced on China: it was followed by similar treaties with the United States, France, Belgium, Sweden, Norway, Portugal, Russia, and Prussia. Up to the 1860s the Western powers were interested mainly in extending trade; after that they were more concerned with colonial acquisitions and by the end of the century it was as common to refer to "German China" (Shandong province) as to speak of "German East Africa" (Franke, 1967a: 70).

The unequal treaties forced on China contained four main points. First, the extraterritoriality of foreigners was established, making them subject to their own law rather than to Chinese law. Second, the level of the customs duties that China could levy was restricted, making it difficult to protect nascent Chinese manufactures against foreign competition. Third, international settlements and concessions were created in the treaty ports and removed from the jurisdiction of Chinese authorities, while other Chinese territories (like Kowloon, opposite Hong Kong) were leased to foreigners, usually for 99 years. Fourth, foreign ships were granted free movement in Chinese inland and territorial waters. After the Japanese defeated China in the Sino-Japanese War of 1894-1895, Japan won the right to establish manufacturing facilities in the treaty ports. The "most favored nation clause," which the foreign powers forced upon China in their treaties from 1843, automatically extended this right to all the others, for this clause stipulated that any right the Chinese should grant to other nations in the future would be automatically extended to the signatory.

The impact of the West upon Chinese development and underdevelopment was many-faceted. As I shall discuss at some length in the following section, some scholars have attributed Chinese underdevelopment primarily to the impact of Western imperialism, while others have seen the Western impact as the primary stimulus to development. Here I would like mainly to indicate some of the background information that will be helpful in assessing the Western impact.

First, it should be noted that insofar as the West had an economic impact in the nineteenth century it was exerted primarily through trade rather than through direct private investment. It was not until China's defeat in the Sino-Japanese War of 1894-1895 that direct foreign investment in the treaty ports became legal, and except for missionary houses foreigners were never allowed to own real estate outside the treaty ports. Also, foreign borrowing by the Chinese government was limited prior to the Sino-Japanese War, although indemnity payments resulting from the wars launched by the Western powers or imposed by force following attacks by Chinese civilians on foreigners at times put a serous strain on the imperial budget. This strain became steady and severe from the time of the Sino-Japanese War. Trade data appear in Table 1.

After the Sino-Japanese War, direct foreign investment grew rapidly, with the annual average amounting to U.S. $47 million between 1902 and 1913, and increasing to $75.1 million between 1914 and 1930 (Dernberger, 1975: 29). At the same time, debt service on largely nonproductive loans combined with substantial indemnity payments as a consequence mainly of the Boxer "rebellion" in 1900 created steady pressure on the national

TABLE 1
China's Exports, Imports and Total Trade, 1871-1929

(U.S. $ millions; commodity trade only; annual averages) Years	Exports	Imports	Total Trade	Per capita	% of world trade	Exports as % of GDP
1871–84	$102.5	$106.2	$208.7	$0.58	1.3%	2.5%
1885–1900	110.2	143.5	253.7	0.66	1.3	–
1901–14	201.0	293.8	494.8	1.19	1.5	–
1915–19	521.2	570.8	1,092.0	2.47	–	–
1920–29	619.6	799.0	1,418.6	3.01	2.4	7.3

SOURCE: Dernberger (1975: 27).

budget and left little room for discretionary measures in support of industrialization. Between 1929 and 1934, loan and indemnity payments accounted for between 31.8% and 40.5% of national budget expenditures (Lippit, 1974: 156).

While foreign investment expanded quite rapidly in the twentieth century and took a dominant role in a number of industries, Chinese-owned industry also expanded rapidly.[8] "By 1912, there were 20,749 Chinese factories employing seven or more workers. Even in 1933, after the peak of direct foreign investment, Chinese-owned factories in the modern manufacturing sector outnumbered foreign-owned factories by more than ten to one" (Dernberger, 1975: 41). To evaluate the importance of foreign-owned factories by their relative number, however, would be highly misleading, because the average foreign factory was much larger than its Chinese counterpart. Even allowing for this, the data presented in Table 2 indicate that Chinese industrial output was produced mainly in Chinese-owned firms in 1933. Since all modern industry in China had been minimal at the turn of the century, the evidence indicates that Chinese-owned factories were not as a group replaced by foreign ones but grew apace with them. Since the industry in Manchuria was entirely foreign-owned in 1933, the figures for Chinese-owned industry in China proper that appear in Table 2 also indicate the share of

TABLE 2
Output and Number of Workers in Chinese- and
Foreign-Owned Factories, 1933

	Gross value of output (Chin. $ millions)	%	Number of workers (1,000s)	%
China proper				
Chin.-owned	1,771.4	66.9	783.2	72.8
For.-owned	497.4	18.8	163.1	15.2
Manchuria	376.7	14.3	129.5	12.0
Total	2,645.5	100.0	1,075.8	100.0

SOURCE: Feuerwerker (1968: 14).

Chinese-owned industry in China as a whole: 66.9%. Over the entire period between 1912 and 1949, modern industry in China grew at an average annual rate of 5.6% (Chang, 1969: 71).

Like the industrialization of the West and Japan, that of China before 1949 required a labor forced to alienate its labor under abominable conditions merely to subsist. To sustain their labor force employers as a group must typically pay a subsistence wage. While the wage is for an individual worker, however, the subsistence is for a family. The greater the participation of family members in the labor force, therefore, the less that each individual worker can be paid. Moreover, as mechanical power often reduces the physical strength required for productive activity, the growth of modern industry makes more feasible the use of female and child operatives. As elsewhere during the early stages of the industrial revolution, therefore, the typical factory operative in China during the first half of the twentieth century was not a man but a woman or child. Table 3 presents the data based on a comprehensive industrial survey of 1933. The case of an (industrial) tobacco worker in Shanghai, cited by Barnett (1941: 42-43), conveys clearly the sense in which workers could be paid a less-than-subsistence wage when the whole family worked. In 1936 the man in question worked nine and one-half hours a day and received 14.68 yuan per month, or about half of his family's expenses. His wife was employed in a silk-reeling establishment, working an 11-hour day and receiving 10.90 yuan per month. One of his daughters, 16 years old, worked an 11 and one-half hour day in a cotton-spinning mill for 10.05 yuan per

TABLE 3
Factory Employees in Chinese-Owned Factories, 1933

Men	202,762
Women	243,435
Children	47,060

SOURCE: Feuerwerker (1968: 18-19); based on a survey by D. K. Lieu.

month. His younger daughter, 9 years old and small for her age, accompanied his wife to work and in return for her food was permitted to serve an apprenticeship.

> For 11 hours each day this tot stood upon a raised platform wielding a small brush in a steaming brazier full of boiling cocoons. Thus holding his family together in the one room which they occupied, this worker believed himself a lucky man. . . . The sum of his family's collective income in 1936 amounted to Chinese $35.63 each month or, in terms of American dollars, about U.S. $8.90. This was rather more than most of his working associates could boast.

In general, conditions in 1936 were far better than they had been four years earlier, when the worldwide depression was at its worst, or than they would be four years later, when Shanghai reached the peak of a miniboom despite the outbreak of war or because of it as inflation pushed the real wages of workers to 55% of the 1936 level (Barnett, 1941: 53). Quite directly, the situation of workers in Shanghai represented that of workers in China generally, for Shangahi held, in 1934, some 40% of the industrial capital of China excluding Manchuria (seized by the Japanese in 1931), employed 43% of the industrial workers and produced 50% of the industrial output (Barnett, 1941: 76).

Life in the countryside also posed its difficulties. A sophisticated European observer, the missionary Abbé Regis-Evariste Huc, after spending 1839 to 1851 in China and traveling throughout the country, wrote:

> At all epochs, and in the most flourishing and best governed countries, there always have been, and there always will be, poor; but unquestionably there can be found in no other country such a depth of disastrous poverty as in the Celestial Empire. Not a year passes in which a terrific number of persons do not perish of famine in some part or other of China; and the multitude of those who live merely from day to day is incalculable. Let a drought, an inundation, or any accident whatever, occur to injure the harvest in a single province, and two thirds of the population are immediately reduced to a state of starvation. You

see them forming themselves into numerous bands—perfect armies of beggars—and proceeding together, men, women and children, to seek in the towns and villages for some little nourishment wherewith to sustain, for a brief interval, their miserable existence. Many fall down fainting by the wayside, and die before they can reach the place where they had hoped to find help. You see their bodies lying in the fields, and at the roadside, and you pass without taking much notice of them—so familiar is the horrid spectacle [Schurmann and Schell, 1967: 30-31].

It may be that the appalling conditions of rural China a century later were no worse, but they were certainly no better. Life for a majority of the peasants remained marginal. Famine remained endemic. Bandits roamed the countryside and in some places were so well organized and powerful as to place a tax on the harvest. Given a succession of weak and corrupt governments, warlords dominated various regions; in such places as Sichuan they collected taxes many years in advance (Buck, 1968: 328). The central government continued to rely heavily on tax-farming for its revenues; in view of its weakness, those who obtained the rights would squeeze whatever they could obtain from the peasantry, remitting only a small percentage to the government (Chen, 1973: 74). In much of south China at least, tenancy appears to have been increasing. Justice was a luxury of the well-to-do and in every sense the poor and landless peasants were victims. Thus, by the first half of the twentieth century, China had acquired all of the characteristics associated with underdevelopment.

THEORIES OF UNDERDEVELOPMENT

A number of theories have been advanced to explain the development of underdevelopment in China. Although some of them provide insights into the process, none of them is fully satisfactory. For treatment here, I have divided them somewhat arbitrarily into two main groups of three each. The first group includes especially general theories of underdevelopment which I analyze in relation to the Chinese case, except that the first of these, the "pre-industrial stage theory," has already been applied specifically to China by Eckstein, Fairbank, and Yang. The second and third theories in this group treat underdevelopment as a consequence of vicious circles which limit the supply of savings and the demand for investment, and as a consequence of the colonial and imperialist expansion of the West.

The second group of three involves attempts by China-scholars to explain underdevelopment in China specifically. The first of these attempts to ascribe underdevelopment in China to a number of features of the Chinese social structure. Although Levy (1949: 350-365) puts great stress on the Chinese family system as an obstacle to modernization, the emphasis on social structure is not associated with a single thinker and possibly because the case is so weak it has never been fully elaborated. Even so, many writers have emphasized one aspect of traditional Chinese social structure or another as a significant barrier to modernization, so it seems desirable to pay some attention to this issue in a unified fashion. The second theory in this group has received the most sophisticated elaboration. Elvin's theory of the "high-level equilibrium trap" has, moreover, proven so convincing that it has been accepted by many contemporary China scholars, including especially economists, and has even been treated by some as an established fact rather than as an hypothesis. It will be necessary, therefore, to analyze this theory in some detail in order to reveal the shaky grounds upon which it rests. Finally, possibly the most insightful of the theories of China's underdevelopment is that developed by Balazs over the course of his writings. Balazs attributes the failure of modernization in China to the constraints of a bureaucratic state and elite bureaucratic class stifling all private initiative. Despite the validity of many of his observations, his theory is too narrow and cannot explain such central issues as why the structure of the state failed to inhibit expansion in some periods while curtailing it drastically in others.

PREINDUSTRIAL STAGE THEORY

According to a model developed by Eckstein, Fairbank, and Yang, the Chinese case can be fitted into one of two basic patterns of development, a pattern characterized by (1) traditional equilibrium, (2) the rise of disequilibrating forces, (3) gestation, (4) breakthrough or take-off, and (5) self-sustaining growth (Eckstein, 1975: 87-88). These authors argue that in the early nineteenth century China was in a state of "traditional equilibrium." The exogenous shock created by Western expansion in the nineteenth century, combined with population pressure and administrative decay, ushered in "a century-long process of disintegration, transformation and slow gestation within the traditional Chinese order" (Eckstein, 1975: 89-90), during which time

an acute degree of tension, in the minds of proud conservatives and later in the minds of modern patriotic Chinese . . . gradually built up to explosive proportions until the shackles of the old order were violently broken and the Chinese economy erupted at long last into [the] industrial take-off under totalitarian control which we are witnessing today [Eckstein: 90].

According to this stage theory, then, the social and economic institutions of the traditional order blocked development until the advent of the West, after a period of gestation and mental anguish, unleashed the forces of modernization.

Like other stage theories, this one is neither historical nor explanatory.[9] First, it is proper to inquire as to the meaning of a "traditional equilibrium." If it means "preindustrial" equilibrium, then the stages are tautological, for industrialization must be preceded by a period before industrialization and one leading up to it. Whether it does or not, the concept of traditional equilibrium belies the richness of change in "traditional" China. Chinese history is replete with equilibria and disequilibria and enormous economic changes—such as, for example, the commercial revolution in the medieval period, periods of active technological progress and others of relative stagnation, and so forth. Are all of these to be subsumed as part of the "traditional equilibrium?" If the theory is to be made historical, then it will be necessary to speak of "traditional equilibria" rather than a single equilibrium, and once this is done it will be more reasonable to argue that the first three stages have been repeated several times in Chinese history without proceeding to the fourth. A stage theory is of little value unless it can distinguish among stages unambiguously and unless it can clarify the logical necessity according to which each stage gives rise to the subsequent one; this theory fails on both counts.

Furthermore, the concept of "equilibrium" itself can be highly misleading. It can result from the dynamic tension of opposing forces or the absence of tension and opposition. The authors of the preindustrial stage theory imply the latter by suggesting that it is the growing tensions of the gestation period following exogenous shocks that led to industrialization. They strengthen this impression by incorrectly likening ninteenth century China to Malthus's and Ricardo's model of a "stationary state," with a "population pressing against resources close to the margin of subsistence" (Eckstein, 1975: 91). In fact, as I will show below, the Chinese economy produced a considerable surplus above subsistence, and the control and use of this surplus was the central factor determining economic change in "traditional" China. By failing to grasp the role of the surplus and of the class structure associated with it, the authors of the stage theory not only miss the essential domestic forces contributing to underdevelopment in China but even obscure the impact of the West, which can properly be understood only in terms of its interaction with domestic forces.

Thus, the pre-industrial stage theory does little to help us understand underdevelopment in China. By creating a category of "traditional equilibrium" which lumps China together with other contemporary underdeveloped countries, it denies a history to all of them. By treating underdevelopment as a characteristic of traditional society in China, it fails to grasp underdevelopment as a historical *process;* it cannot, accordingly, illuminate the process by which the world's most developed civilization became one of the most underdeveloped. Lacking any substantive explanation of the development of underdevelopment in China and lumping all social forces into a traditional equilibrium inimical to growth, Eckstein, Fairbank, and Yang must explain modernization as a response to exogenous forces. Thus their theory of stages fails to go beyond its own initial assumptions.

THE VICIOUS CIRCLE OF POVERTY THESIS

The vicious circle of poverty thesis is another attempt to explain the phenomenon of underdevelopment generally. The theory has been most articulately stated by Nurkse (1964) in his classical work, *Problems of Capital Formation in Underdeveloped Countries.* Nurkse identifies two primary vicious circles, one limiting the demand for investment, the other the supply of savings. The poverty of the less developed countries is common to both of them. In poor countries, people's income is low and their purchasing power limited. This in turn limits the size of the market, making investment unattractive and limiting the demand for capital to invest. The limited amount of capital formation that results limits worker productivity and keeps incomes low, thus perpetuating the circle. On the supply of savings side, which Nurske regards as more critical, low incomes limit the capacity to save, restricting the availability of capital for investment purposes. Again the limited capital stock per worker that results limits productivity and keeps incomes low, thereby perpetuating the circle.

While Nurkse's analysis does help to identify several of the critical problems of the development process, it explains neither underdevelopment in general nor the Chinese case in particular. It might first be noted that not everyone in poor countries is poor. Since one's ability to save depends, for the most part, on one's relative income standing within a referent group rather than on the absolute income level, even the poorest underdeveloped countries tend to have a substantial if usually untapped savings potential. On the demand for investment side, most countries have markets large enough to sustain at least some industrial development in such fields as brewing, baking, the manufacture of soap, matches, cloth, and so forth. The rise in productivity and incomes in such industries as these can help sustain the development of markets in other industries.

I have already noted the relatively extensive development of markets in premodern China. The typical farm family was by no means a subsistence producer, and in this sense the often-recreated image of China's premodern economy as a "cellular" one is somewhat misleading. In late imperial China as a whole, between 20% and 30% of agricultural output was marketed (Feuerwerker, 1976b: 86), with the proportion rising to between 30% and 40% in the twentieth century (Perkins, 1969: 115), with a much higher figure characteristic of certain regions. A number of industrial products enjoyed a national and even international market. "By the K'ang-hsi period (1662-1722), when Chinese porcelain 'had materially altered' the artistic tastes of the English aristocracy, the Ching-te borough (in northern Kiangsi) had about five hundred procelain furnaces working day and night to meet the national and foreign demand" (Ho, 1959: 201). In general, considerable regional specialization in production developed in premodern China, with interregional and local trade focusing on such staple commodities as grain, salt, fish, drugs, timber, hardware, potteries, and cloths, together with a variety of luxury goods for the ruling classes (Ho, 1959: 198-199). During the late Ming and early Qing periods especially, the rise of interregional trade is attested to by the growing number of merchant guildhalls established in commercial centers. The lack of markets cannot have been a depressant on the demand for investment in premodern China.

At the same time, we know that poverty was not an absolute constraint on the ability to save in China. Ho Ping-ti (1959: 197) cities the account of Xie Zhao-zhe, a Chinese official writing in 1602:

The rich men of the empire in the regions south of the Yangtze are from Hui-chou (southern Anhwei), in the regions north of the river from Shansi. The great merchants of Hui-chou take fisheries and salt as their occupation and have amassed fortunes amounting to one million taels of silver. Others with a fortune of two or three hundred thousands can only rank as middle merchants. The Shansi merchants are engaged in salt, or silk, or reselling, or grain. Their wealth even exceeds that of the former.

In general, the late Ming-early Qing period was marked by the rise of great merchants. But the amassing of great fortunes was also an official prerogative and continued throughout Chinese history. According to Fairbank (1971: 104),

High office commonly meant riches. The favorite minister of the Ch'ien-lung Emperor, when tried for corruption and other crimes by that Emperor's successor in 1799, was found to have an estate worth in our terms of that period more than one billion-dollars— probably an all-time record. Another high Manchu, who fell into disfavor at the time of the Opium War in 1841, was found to have an estate of some 425,000 acres of land, $30,000,000 worth of gold, silver, and precious stones, and shares in 90 banks and pawnshops.

Another way of grasping the savings potential of premodern China is to estimate the size of the surplus above the population's subsistence requirements. According to the estimates of Riskin (1975: 74), this figure was 27.2% of net domestic product in the 1930s, and the discussion in the final section of the present article suggests that for the late nineteenth century, the surplus was at least 30% of national income, again indicating that there was no absolute lack of savings capacity. Thus, it is clear that China's failure to develop vigorously between the ending of the medieval economic revolution and 1949 can be ascribed neither to the absence of markets nor to the absence of capital.

COLONIALISM AND IMPERIALISM

The emerging radical paradigm in development economics regards underdevelopment as essentially a historical process created by the imperialist-colonial expansion of the West. Unlike the orthodox paradigm, which treats trade, aid and contact with the West as stimuli for development through the infusion of capital and new technology, the radical paradigm regards such relations as tending to promote underdevelopment, a consequence of the extraction of the resources and surplus of the less developed countries to serve the purposes of the advanced or advancing countries, the growth of technological, financial, and cultural dependency, and the support afforded elite classes opposed to the basic changes necessary for development.[10] Above all, the radical paradigm breaks sharply with the orthodox paradigm's tendency to deny underdeveloped countries a history (by treating them all simply as "preindustrial"), emphasizing by contrast that underdevelopment is a historical process. The concept of "development of underdevelopment," from which the title of this study is derived, stresses that underdevelopment is not an inherent characteristic of preindustrial societies but one which has emerged as a consequence of specific historical forces.[11]

In this sense, I believe that the radical paradigm has much to offer students of economic development. Ultimately, however, in the form in which it has usually been articulated—treating underdevelopment as a consequence of the same historical forces which gave rise to development in the West—the radical paradigm cannot provide a sufficient explanation of the development of underdevelopment in China.

In many ways, the work of Baran is the starting point of the counter-paradigm. In *The Political Economy of Growth* (1968: 145-146), he includes a description of the manner in which the promising development of eighteenth century India was choked off by British colonial rule. He sees the process as characterized by a transfer of the economic surplus from India to England, India's inability under British rule to protect its own markets, severe restrictions on the import of technology, and exclusion from export markets in Britain and elsewhere. Writing in the same tradition, Frank (1973: 95) sees underdevelopment as "in large part the historical product of past and continuing economic and other relations between the satellite underdeveloped and the now developed metropolitan countries," while Griffin (1973: 69) argues that "the automatic functioning of the international economy which Europe dominated first created underdevelopment and then hindered efforts to escape from it." To what extent then, can underdevelopment in China be understood as a consequence of Western expansion?

I would like to argue here that although the imperialist-colonial behavior of the West (including Japan) was, on balance, inimical to Chinese development,[12] the primary role in the development of underdevelopment cannot be ascribed to it. This may be done most reasonably by first noting the ways in which Western actions contributed to underdevelopment in China and then arguing that the principal features of underdevelopment appeared and were sustained independently, for the most part, of the Western impact. The limited contribution of the West to the development of underdevelopment in China is not because the intentions of the West were innocent—just the opposite is true—but because the process had deeper roots in the domestic economy.

There is no easy way to assess quantitatively the importance of the West's forcing opium upon China, but there can be no doubt that it did great harm. Opium was the leading import into China through most of the nineteenth century and was not edged out by cotton piece goods until about 1890 (Feuerwerker, 1969: 52), by which time China was able to supply most of its own needs. Indeed, opium became the first major case of import-substitution based "development"; by the end of the century 10% of the Chinese population was smoking opium (Spence, 1975: 154). Not only did the opium trade drain a substantial portion of the economic surplus out of China, the impetus it gave to organized crime and official corruption was, like the creation of a nation of addicts, hardly conducive to development. There is perhaps no more dramatic instance of the hypocrisy of Western proclamations of superior civilization than the opium trade the West foisted upon China, and it would be interesting to know what

support a general theory of rural decline in response to the Western impact.

In Chinese manufacturing, a parallel argument can be made. Japanese textile firms in China, although vigorous competitors among themselves, did engage in collusion on prices and other matters through regular meetings in order to drive Chinese competitors out of business, while the foreign-owned utilities gave preference to foreign enterprises in providing power and other products (Kiyokawa, 1975). As in the case of handicrafts, however, when the case studies and general observations are supplemented by the aggregate evidence, a rather contradictory picture emerges, for the Chinese firms as a group grew as fast as the Western ones. In large-scale manufacturing as a whole, for example, including firms with 30 or more employees and using power, the share of foreign firms was 35% in 1936 and that of Chinese firms, 65% (Hou, 1965: 129). While we lack earlier figures with which to compare these, given the initiative taken by foreign firms in the establishment of most modern industries, it appears that Chinese firms were at least able to hold their own and may have increased their share of the total over time. This is not to deny that foreigners held a dominant role in the modern sector generally and especially in strategic areas like mining, heavy industry, and shipping, but simply to point out that this dominance did not preclude a comparable growth of Chinese-owned industry.

With regard to financial matters, the case against the foreign impact is much stronger. As has been true in the less developed countries generally, foreign firms financed much of their expansion with retained earnings and locally generated capital, and the new capital inflow was more than offset by larger remittances abroad of profit, interest, and capital. Moreover, payments by the Chinese government on foreign loans and indemnities consistently exceeded the proceeds from new loans. Thus, at least from the beginning of the twentieth century, the Western impact tended to drain the surplus out of China. The annual inpayments and outpayments on foreign investments in China appear in Table 4. These figures suggest that the West was indeed extracting

TABLE 4

Annual Inpayments and Outpayments on Foreign Investments in China,
1894-1936 (Chin $ millions)

Period	Inpayments			Outpayments			Inpayment-Outpayment ratios (percent)		
	Govt. loans	Direct invest- ment	Total	Govt. loans	Direct invest- ment	Total	Govt. loans	Direct invest- ment	Total
1894-1901	21.3	-	-	20.9	-	-	101.9	-	-
1902-1913	61.0	52.8	113.8	89.2	69.3	158.5	68.4	76.2	71.8
1914-1930	23.8	73.6	97.4	70.9	138.8	209.7	33.6	53.0	46.5
1928	4.0	96.0	100.0	63.0	179.0	242.0	6.35	53.63	41.3
1929	0.0	170.0	170.0	79.1	198.5	277.6	0.0	85.6	61.2
1930	0.0	202.0	202.0	111.4	198.0	309.4	0.0	101.8	65.3
1931	-	-	43.6	135.2	87.2	222.4	-	-	19.6
1932	-	-	60.0	90.0	56.0	146.0	-	-	41.1
1933	-	-	30.0	93.0	24.0	117.0	-	-	26.6
1934	-	-	80.0	112.6	15.0	127.6	-	-	54.9
1935	-	-	140.0	107.4	55.0	162.4	-	-	86.2
1936	-	-	60.0	127.8	70.0	197.8	-	-	30.3

SOURCE: Hou (1965: 99-100).
NOTE: The data exclude Manchuria after 1931.

the surplus from China rather than providing fresh capital on a net basis. The critical question with regard to this, however, is whether the portion of the surplus that drained out of the country would have made a substantive contribution to development had it not done so. Since the amounts going abroad were an extremely small share of the total surplus—slightly over 1% in 1933, for example, based on Table 4 and the 7.85 billion yuan estimate of the actual surplus which appears in the section below entitled, "The high-level equilibrium trap"—and since a minimal share of the domestically retained surplus went into investment or development-related projects, it appears unlikely that terminating the foreign drain on China's resources could in itself have provided a major thrust for modernization.

In assessing the impact of Western colonialism and imperialism on Chinese underdevelopment, the effect of foreign control over Chinese tariffs and support for a government which hindered modernization must also be considered. An Englishman was placed in charge of the Chinese customs bureau from 1854, and tariffs were limited to 5% of the value of imported goods.

Tariff autonomy was not fully regained until 1929, when the ratio of the actual import duty to total import value was 8.5%; it rose steeply thereafter to 29.7% in 1936 (Hou, 1965: 108). It is evident that the tariff restrictions prevented the Chinese government from protecting nascent industries against foreign competition. Against this, however, must be weighed a number of considerations which in the aggregate suggest that foreign control of the customs was not seriously inimical to Chinese development.

While budgetary problems would have been magnified, there was nothing to prevent the Chinese government from subsidizing selected industries directly as a substitute for tariff protection until they were capable of meeting foreign competition. Furthermore, government corruption was endemic in Republican as well as Qing times; the honest administration of the customs under foreign control undoubtedly precluded a vast new source of corruption and smuggling, while providing a secure and growing portion of the national budget. It should also be noted that those countries, especially in Latin America, that have tried to base their development on an import-substitution strategy, relying on high tariffs to protect the new industries, have often run into severe problems; the protected industries have typically failed to become internationally competitive, remaining instead inefficient, high-cost producers profiting from their monopolistic-oligopolistic position and imposing excessively high prices on the local population. As I shall argue below, the nature of the traditional state involvement in the Chinese economy would have made such a scenario more than likely if infant-industry protection had been possible. Finally, and most decisively, China showed no signs of a vigorous industrial development policy prior to 1949. Tariff protection might have been justified only in the context of a concerted development strategy. In the absence of one, it is difficult to ascribe great significance to the lack of tariff autonomy as a cause of underdevelopment.

The question of the influence of foreign support for an anachronistic imperial government is also a complex one, but on balance the evidence does not suggest that such support was decisive in perpetuating the dynasty and thereby creating under-development. One of the central issues here is the role of foreigners in suppressing the Taiping Revolution (1850-1864). The Taiping Revolution, supported by a utopian socialist ideology, sought to eradicate the scholar-official and landlord class, together with the Confucian ethos on which its authority rested. According to the Taiping program, private property was to be eliminated and land divided equally for use; men and women were to get an equal share (indeed, the Taiping Revolution was the first great move-ment to raise the issue of women's equality in China) and children under 16, one-half the adult allotment.[13] Each person was entitled to take from the harvest only what was required for his or her own subsistence—everything else was to go into the common granary. Other agricultural products and handicraft products were to be distributed in like fashion. Although the program could not be implemented under the conditions of civil war, its thrust was clear.

By contrast, Zeng Guo-fan, whose army defeated the Taipings, "certainly represented the interests of the landholding Hunan gentry, which strongly resisted the Taipings' revolutionary program—indeed, he had been able to set up and maintain his army only because of the material and spiritual support of the Hunan gentry" (Franke, 1967b: 184). While there was at first considerable popular sentiment abroad in favor of the Taipings on account of their pseudo-Christian ideology, their revolution-ary thrust and the character of their religious claims (Hong Xiu-quan, the leader of the revolution, believed himself to be the son of God and the younger brother of Jesus Christ) soon led to a reversal of sentiment. Eventually, European and especially American mercenaries played an important role in the suppres-sion of the Taipings. On the level of national policy, England and France came to oppose the Taipings for fear that their treaty gains of 1858—especially military reparations and the oppor-tunity to reap opium profits (Taiping commandments banned opium smoking)—would be lost. If indeed the Taipings had had a viable program and the Western opposition had been decisive in their defeat, a strong case could be made on such grounds alone for assigning the responsibility for Chinese underdevelopment to the West.

Neither assumption, however, is correct, as the course of events shows. The Taiping Revolution got under way in Guangxi (south China) in the summer of 1850, with the main support provided by poor peasants and, to a much lesser extent, members of the proletariat, including several hundred charcoal burners, some thousands of mine workers, and coolies from Guangzhou who had lost their jobs as a consequence of the Opium War (Franke, 1967b: 183). Unemployed pirates, deserters from the government and a few businessmen, rich peasants, and scholars also joined the movement. The Revolution rapidly gained strength and in the spring of 1853 the Taipings captured Nanjing, southern capital of the Ming dynasty, after an eleven-day siege. There they temporarily established their capital. When they sent an army north to capture Beijing, the Manchu government prepared to flee, but the thrust fell short due largely to inadequate preparation and poor communications. At about the same time, Hong Xiu-quan (who had had himself declared the Heavenly King) and other leaders entered into a life of excess—including high living, luxury, and many concubines—in direct opposition to the revolutionary code. In Nanjing, bloody internal conflicts developed, leading in 1856 to the deaths of some of the movement's most important leaders, their followers, and twenty or thirty thousand others. With the corruption and decay at the top, the Revolution lost its élan and remained on the defensive from 1856 until it was finally crushed by the capture of Nanjing by Zeng Guo-fan's forces in the summer of 1864.

It is clear that although the Taiping Revolution was essentially a class conflict, the movement lacked class consciousness, and its religious mysticism, opportunism, and other extraneous elements undercut its socialist ideology and created the basis for its internal decay. The failure of the Revolution must be ascribed as much to its internal contradictions as to the gentry-class opposition to its radical objectives. The West, of course, was not responsible for the internal contradictions and although it supported the counterrevolution, its role in it was not primary. Thus, the perpetuation of the Qing dynasty and a government incapable of taking the lead in bringing about China's modernization which the defeat of the Taipings temporarily assured cannot be ascribed to the West.

After the Taiping Revolution, British diplomats feared nothing so much as the collapse of China's weakened central government. Such a collapse, they believed, would make it necessary for the British to step in and assume administrative control over most of China in order to keep it out of the hands of other foreign powers, and they believed that the costs of such administrative control would be out of all proportion to the benefits received (Franke, 1967a: 89-90). Thus the principal aim of British policy became the preservation and strengthening of the central government. In the current age of neocolonialism, it has become clear that one of the basic factors contributing to underdevelopment is foreign sponsorship of governments and class interests inherently opposed to development. If the British had indeed been responsible for perpetuating the imperial regime, their role in China's underdevelopment would be established. In fact, however, revolutionary energies were exhausted for some time after the collapse of the gigantic Taiping effort and the loss of some 20 million lives in the civil war it brought, and there was no severe challenge to the central government until the end of the century. Thus, Western support for reactionary government in China was not decisive in inhibiting economic development.

In making an overall assessment of the impact of the West on the development of underdevelopment in China, one of the most basic questions to consider is whether China showed signs of a vigorous development cut short by the Western impact. Perhaps because the villainous intent of the West is so apparent, it is easy to ascribe excessive importance to the Western impact. Britain fought the Opium War in order to force opium—and anything else it wanted—on China. But if we look at the aftermath of the war, we find that Britain spent most of the remainder of the 1840s trying merely to negotiate entry into the city of Guangzhou for the purpose of trade (Wakeman, 1966: ch. 1). Facts like this must be kept in mind in order to realize that the foreign impact on the economic life of the Chinese was in many ways quite marginal. Foreigners were limited to the treaty ports (except for the missionaries) and could not own real estate outside of them. Until 1895 they could not set up manufacturing facilities even in the treaty ports. Foreign trade was a small share of China's national product (see Table 1), and Chinese always took the role of middleman in trade, keeping some of the gains of trade in Chinese hands. In the twentieth century, a principal source of Chinese industrial capital—which, as I have indicated, held its own with foreign capital—was the profits obtained by the compradores, the Chinese who served as agents for Western firms. I do not mean to suggest here that the Western impact was unimportant, but merely that it should not be exaggerated.

The much more central issue is whether China would have developed in the absence of the Western impact. I believe that the evidence here is quite unambiguous: nineteenth century China showed no signs of the economic vitality that might have made development possible. It is for this reason above all that the impact of the West cannot be assigned primary responsibility for the development of underdevelopment in China. In presenting my own understanding of the development of underdevelopment in China later in this study, I will analyze in some detail the domestic forces responsible; let it suffice here to observe that they must be considered primary and the foreign impact secondary.

SOCIAL STRUCTURE AND UNDERDEVELOPMENT

It has sometimes been argued that various aspects of Chinese social structure have contributed significantly to China's underdevelopment. The particularistic loyalties of the Chinese "family system," for example, have been regarded as fundamental obstacles to development (Levy, 1949), as has the value placed upon classical learning and the scorn with which the elite regarded the practical-minded and the nouveau riche. The case is such a weak one that it would not warrant consideration were it not for the fact that such arguments crop up with embarrassing frequency in the writings of otherwise respectable scholars. Thus I would like here to present a few specific examples of the use and abuse of such arguments and to indicate quite briefly the general grounds on which they must be rejected.

Ho Ping-ti (1959: 205), in an otherwise sophisticated discussion of the shortcomings of China's traditional economy, writes:

> The lack of primogeniture and the working of the clan system proved to be great leveling factors in the Chinese economy. The virtue of sharing one's wealth with one's immediate and remote kinsmen had been so highly extolled since the rise of the Neo-Confucianism in the eleventh and twelfth centuries that few wealthy men in traditional China could escape the influence of this teaching. Business management, in the last analysis, was an extension of familism and was filled with nepotism, inefficiencies and irrationalities. These immensely rich individuals not only failed to develop a capitalistic system; they seldom if ever acquired that acquisitive and competitive spirit which is the very soul of the capitalistic system.

Now we might note that the family plays a central role in the business activity of many premodern societies, some of which have developed and others of which have not. Furthermore, essentially the same family system has existed in oversees Chinese communities, which have been noted for their business leadership throughout much of southeast Asia, and remains strong if modified in modern Hong Kong and Taiwan, both of which have been growing quite rapidly.

In addition, without denying the importance of the family system, we have numerous instances of Chinese business organization transcending it when required by the scale of the activity involved. During the eleventh century, for example, the extensive coastal and international shipping trade was often carried on by several persons in partnership, by many small investors who provided capital to merchants engaged in international trade, or by large merchants who built up trading fleets of as many as 80 ships under delegated managers (Elvin, 1973: 143-144). Another example is provided by the Shanxi banks, established during the eighteenth century for transmitting funds from one locale to another. The eight largest such banks had more than 30 branches each, enabling them to transmit funds from one end of the country to another; in the later nineteenth century they also set up branches in Japan, Singapore, and Russia (Elvin, 1973: 296-297). Although dominated by a few powerful families, these banks were organized as partnerships with unlimited liability for all partners and profits distributed at three- or four-year intervals. Given the multiplicity of examples like these, it is clear that the family system did not necessarily curtail the scope or scale of business activity. It might be added that it is often as appropriate to think of the family arrangements as a convenience for carrying out business activities (family members might be more trustworthy or work harder than others) as to emphasize the possibilities of "nepotism, inefficiencies and irrationalities."

In addition to questioning the family system's supposed role as an organizational constraint on development, it is also proper to question its supposed role as a financial constraint. As numerous fortunes have been built up throughout Chinese history on the basis of official position or commercial activity, it is not at all clear why the same obligation to share with one's relations which failed to preclude the accumulation of fortunes should be blamed for their dissipation. Finally, Ho Ping-ti's suggestion that lack of acquisitiveness on the part of rich people played a role in the failure of China to develop a "genuine capitalistic system" is highly questionable.

In general, it is well to be suspicious of any arguments which assign the responsibility for China's failure to develop to the "wrong" values, lack of acquisitiveness, lack of entrepreneurship, lack of interest in technology or other purported features of China's traditional social structure. China has always been filled with acquisitive people—great fortunes or even small ones were never built up by people lacking in acquisitiveness—and entrepreneurial talents have never been lacking. Furthermore, while the power and prestige of the scholar-officials were much greater than those of even the successful merchants, the initially symbiotic and ultimately still closer relationship between these two classes must be recognized and the pitfall of assuming that the values of one precluded those of the other must be avoided. The merchants used their wealth to acquire the education their progeny would require to enter the class of officials or, especially during the Qing dynasty when the always endemic corruption reached new heights, to purchase official titles or positions directly. Official status was valued in part because it protected one's family's wealth from the depredations of officials or provided the basis for accumulation via the common bribery and extortion, and in part because mercantile success depended on official connections.

Since the training of the scholar-officials and the examinations that certified them were in the classics, it is sometimes asserted that a lack of interest in technology resulted which undermined the possibilities of modernization. While it is true that inadequate attention was paid to matters of technology in late tradtional China—inadequate from the standpoint of the demands of modernization—the low regard in which technology was held cannot properly be abstracted from the class structure and production relations of late traditional China, which awarded wealth, power, and prestige to an elite gentry class that had little or nothing to do with production itself. It is within this more basic context that the low esteem for technology must be grasped, a matter to which I will return in the final section.

THE HIGH-LEVEL EQUILIBRIUM TRAP

The most influential of the modern theories of underdevelopment in China is Elvin's theory of the high level equilibrium trap (1973: ch. 17). Elvin's theory is essentially a variant of Schultz's argument in *Transforming Traditional Agriculture* (1964), where Schultz argues that "traditional" agricultural systems tend to reach a point of sharply diminishing returns to all available inputs. More investment does not take place because it is not profitable, and production remains stagnant. Such a traditional system cannot be transformed by marginal changes, but requires a package of "modern" inputs applied by a farm labor force with the education and skills needed to see the need for them and to apply them. Elvin is concerned with this transformation process only tangentially—when he argues that the West provided the exogeneous shock necessary to free China from the "high-level equilibrium trap" into which reliance on its traditional technology had led. His main concern is with explaining the development of underdevelopment in China in terms of the "trap."

According to Elvin, by late traditional times the big technological advances in traditional agriculture, transport, and so forth "had, as it were, already been used up" (1973: 306). In agriculture,

> Yields per acre were very nearly as high as was possible without the use of advanced industrial-scientific inputs such as selected seeds, chemical fertilizers and pesticides, machinery and pumps powered by the internal combustion engine or electricity, concrete and so on. Furthermore, there was not enough suitable land to raise the yields per worker for the Chinese labour force as a whole by using either eighteenth-century British techniques, which depended critically on the interdependence of crop-raising and animal husbandry, or nineteenth-century American techniques of extensive, low per-acre yield, mechanized cultivation.

> Traditional inputs, whether in the form of irrigation works, fertilizer or labour, were also nearly as high as they could be without running into sharply diminishing, or even negative, returns [Elvin, 1973: 306].

Thus, Elvin claims that sharply diminishing returns for all available inputs characterized Chinese agriculture in late traditional times. Earlier advances had made Chinese agriculture quite sophisticated (and yields per acre were quite high) within the constraints of a premodern system, but the difficulty of further advance combined with the steady growth of population left the Chinese economy in a high-level equilibrium trap "that was amost incapable of change through internally-generated forces"

(1972: 312). Elvin understands the development of underdevelopment in China, then, as essentially the result of technological and resource constraints exacerbated by population pressures. Since his theory has had so much influence, I would like to indicate some of this before turning to a more formal exposition of his model and a discussion of the decisive reasons for rejecting his theory.

Dernberger (1975: 26) treats the high-level equilibrium trap thesis as a "given," and uses it to support his argument that the foreigner cannot have been the primary cause of China's agricultural problems. Without challenging his conclusion, I would like to note that the equilibrium trap theory rests on tenuous grounds and cannot be regarded as a "given" or the basis for rejecting alternative explanations of China's underdevelopment. In the same volume of essays, Perkins (1975: 120) accepts a variant of the equilibrium trap thesis in arguing that "China's traditional agriculture did not reach the complete stagnation of a 'high-level equilibrium trap' until after the mid-point of the twentieth century."

Elvin's formal exposition of the high-level trap is carried out with the aid of a figure reproduced here as Figure 1. The curve OT shows how output would increase as labor inputs are added to a given quantity of land if the best premodern techniques were used; its curved shape reflects the diminishing returns to equal increments of the variable input, labor. The curves P_1, P_2, and so on reflect different levels of practice or technology in general use; they too reflect diminishing returns. At any given time, output can be increased by increasing labor inputs (as long as the output curve is still rising or the marginal product of labor is positive) or, more significantly, by improving the level of practice. OS shows subsistence requirements, assuming, not unreasonably, that these are directly proportional to the size of the labor force.

When the labor force is OD, the actual level of output is OB, the actual surplus above subsistence BC, and the potential surplus AC. The existence of a surplus makes possible net investment which, together with changes in organization (Elvin cites com-

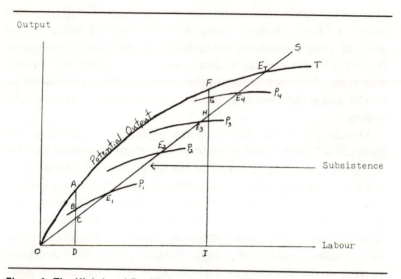

Figure 1: The High-Level Equilibrium Trap in Agriculture
SOURCE: Elvin (1973: 313)

mercialization and land tenure in particular) make possible a shift to a higher level of practice. This procedure can continue until E_T is reached, when there is no longer a surplus and when the best premodern methods are already in use. At that point the traditional economy will have exhausted its potentialities for internally generated development: it is caught in a trap. Elvin believes that by the late eighteenth century China was caught in such a trap, Dernberger ascribes it to the end of the nineteenth century, and Perkins sees it as fully operative soon after the middle of the twentieth century.

Despite the impressive paraphernalia used in its exposition, the high-level equilibrium trap theory has several major deficiencies which render it more obscurantist than explanatory. Possibly the first thing that must be questioned is whether there is indeed such a sharp dichotomy between premodern and modern techniques as to create an unavoidable discontinuity in technological progress. The theory assumes an inverse correlation for the traditional economy between the level of technology and the possibilities for improving it, and Elvin's reference to "improvements in late traditional agricultural technology" reaching "a point of sharply diminishing returns" (p. 306) makes this quite explicit. The deficiencies in his argument are reminiscent of those of Malthus. The law of diminishing returns refers to changes in output as one or more inputs are increased and at least one held constant for a given technology; there is no law that can be applied to the rate of technological progress and it is improper to speak of the best inventions having been "used up."

Second, the theory assumes a Chinese insularity that must in fact be explained. Many of the inventions and innovations of the West in the later eighteenth and early nineteenth centuries could have contributed decidely to Chinese economic progress. For example, James Watt's development of the steam engine came about through his efforts to improve upon the Newcomen engine for pumping out mines and forestalling flooding. Given the critical importance of water conservancy in Chinese agriculture, there was an obvious rationale for the adoption and adaptation of Watt's engine, the use of which would have provided clear stimulus to further industrialization. To speak of China as being in a trap, therefore, is highly misleading. Rather, we must ask why China failed to investigate and make use of the technology available in the West, why nothing even remotely akin to the veritable explosion of technological borrowing that characterized Meiji Japan, for example, took place.

One of the principal defects of the "trap" thesis is its assertion that the surplus above subsistence disappeared. As investment must come out of the surplus, and as new technology must typically be embodied in the form of new investment, the elimination of the surplus had it occurred would assuredly have hindered development. In fact, however, the surplus was not eliminated. As I have shown elsewhere, using the capital share of national income as a proxy for the surplus, the surplus generated in the agricultural sector alone came to at least 16.9% of national income in 1933 excluding taxes, and 19.0% including taxes paid by the owner-operators of farms (Lippit, 1974: 76 and ch. 2). The surplus here includes land rent (10.7% of national income), the surplus produced by annually hired labor above its own consumption (3.4%), and rural interest payments (2.8%), but excludes the special levies of the government, the depredations of warlords and bandits, and so forth, all of which were considerable but which are difficult to quantify with any precision.

In an excellent study, Riskin (1975: 74) has shown that the industrial sector generated an additional 8.2% of national income, so that the capital share or surplus came to some 27.2% of national income in 1933 for the economy as a whole (or 7.85 billion yuan out of a 1933 net domestic product of 28.86 billion yuan; Liu, and Yeh, 1965: 66): the proportion of surplus increases to 36.8% if the potential surplus, including the output foregone due to unemployed and unutilized resources, is calculated. Further analysis presented below suggests that if the conservative bias in the estimates of Riskin and myself is recognized (especially the exclusion of those components of the surplus that are not readily quantifiable), then the surplus in nineteenth century China cannot have been less than 30% of the national income. Since the surplus was so large, it is clear that the Chinese economy was by no means "trapped." Indeed, the central question we must ask is why, given the substantial investment potential indicated by the size of the surplus, so little investment, modernization, and technical progress actually took place. This question can be answered only by examining the class structure and uses of the surplus in late traditional times, a task to which I shall turn in the final section below.

There is no evidence to show a declining surplus in the first half of the twentieth century and nothing to prove a secular decline between Song or early Ming and late traditional times. What little evidence we have, in fact, suggests that the size of the surplus did not change very much. For example, the share of rent in the agricultural output of tenant farmers is an indicator of the size of the surplus. Ordinarily, the tenant must receive at least a subsistence income and the surplus remaining defines the maximum limit of the rental share (the rental share may be smaller than this maximum if the number of people willing to work as tenants is limited in relation to the landowner demand for their services). If the surplus were declining over time, one would expect to find a secular decline in rent levels. However, in Song times the serfs and tenants paid about 50% of the harvest as rent (Balazs, 1972: 120), a figure which held through Ming and Qing times (Perkins, 1969: 20), and indeed right through the first half of the twentieth century (Lippit, 1974: 45-63). While the rental evidence cannot be considered conclusive, it strongly suggests that if anything the agricultural surplus tended to remain roughly constant over time.

Finally, the high-level equilibrium trap theory seems to put an excessive burden on agriculture (and to a lesser extent, transport) as the leading sector in modernization. While the importance of the agricultural sector should be recognized, this sector is by no means necessarily or even usually the leading sector in modernization. Changes in the industrial sector can bring about the modernization of agriculture as well as of industry and the trap theory diverts attention from this central point. Elvin does argue correctly that the organization of many of the principal handicraft activities as part-time activities of rural households tended to discourage innovation by making supply highly elastic at low prices. This was not, however, an absolute barrier to innovation, as the eventual mechanization of spinning proved, and many industries were not so organized. There is, moreover, no sense in which urban-based or new industries would have been subject to the trap. There is no reasonable basis, therefore, for applying the concept of a trap to the industrial sector. And if progress in the industrial sector could have led to the transformation of the agricultural sector, then the agricultural sector and the economy as a whole can scarcely be considered to have been "trapped." Far from clarifying the development of underdevelopment in China, then, the high-level equilibrium trap theory has diverted attention from the central issues. It is not correct to assert that invention and innovation were precluded by technological constraints and population pressures in late traditional China; rather we must be concerned with the nature of the economic, social, and political forces which interacted to preclude development.

BALAZS'S THEORY OF THE BUREAUCRATIC STATE

According to Balazs, the failure of industrial capitalism to develop in China despite highly favorable conditions—China was ahead of the West technologically and scientifically until the time of the Renaissance—was due to the stifling effect of the bureaucratic state. Balazs writes (1972: 11),

> Chinese ingenuity and inventiveness . . . would no doubt have continued to enrich China and would probably have brought it to the threshold of the industrial age, if they had not been stifled by state control. It was the state that killed technological invention in China.

He understands the inhibiting role of the state in the context of class relations, viewing the dominant scholar-official class, a class which "possessed every privilege, above all the privilege of reproducing itself, because of its monopoly of education," as "the embodiment of the state, which was created in [its] image—a hierarchical, authoritarian state" (pp. 16-17). This was a state so strong that the merchant class

> never dared to fight it openly in order to extract from it liberties, laws, and autonomy for themselves. Chinese businessmen almost always preferred to reach a compromise rather than fight, to imitate rather than branch out on their own, to invest money safely in land and carry on the permitted form of usury rather than risk putting their money into industrial enterprises. Their abiding ideal was to become assimilated, to be part of the state by becoming—or seeing their children or grandchildren become— scholar-officials themselves.

> Every time the merchant class succeeded in attaining some degree of liberty, or arrogating to itself some right, or securing an advantage, the state intervened, curtailed the liberty, and arbitrarily

took over, wiping out the advantages gained. The merchant class for its part ... always chose to haggle rather than fight. ... Whenever a new invention (printing, bills of exchange, paper money, water mills) made its appearance in circles which the scholar-officials regarded as hostile, they sooner or later seized it in order to profit from it at the expense of the inventors, who were dismissed from the scene. As a result of this recurring process the scholar-officials and the merchants formed two hostile but interdependent classes. There was an interpenetration, a symbiosis, between them: the scholar-official became "bourgeoisified," while the merchant's ambition turned to becoming a scholar-official and investing his profits in land. Their common ground was that peculiarly Chinese phenomenon, corruption, and their normal reciprocal relationship might be described as one of bully-squeeze [Balazs, 1972: 23, 32].

It will be clear from the foregoing passages that Balazs's understanding of the development of underdevelopment in China is quite different from that of the other authors I have discussed. His theory makes important contributions to our understanding of the development of underdevelopment in China, and I would like to comment on these briefly before turning to a critique of his analysis.

Balazs is correct in calling our attention to the primacy of internal factors inhibiting development, in perceiving that these were primarily social rather than technological, and above all in grasping the importance of class relations. In considering the stability and perpetuation of any economic system, possibly the first question that must be asked is "Who benefits from it?" When we speak of "China" as though it were integral in every respect we are in one sense creating a metaphysical entity, for "China," like other countries, is or has been composed of groups and classes with sharply differing perspectives and interests. In explaining why China did not develop, we must recognize the possibility that development might not have been advantageous to the dominant classes or groups, that development did not take place because these did not *want* development to take place. Indeed, if a dominant class felt, as the Qian Long Emperor stated in his memorial to King George, that it had everything it wanted, it would be quite natural for it to actively oppose development and development-related measures as threats to its position. As Baran (1968: 3-4) succinctly states, "Economic development has always been propelled by classes and groups interested in the new economic and social order, has always been opposed and obstructed by those interested in the preservation of the *status quo*." The principal merit of Balazs's theory is in calling to our attention the central role played by the class structure of traditional China in preventing modernization. His description (p. 154) of the scholar-gentry class helps to explain its interest in preserving the traditional system.

> The Chinese official—the dominant, central figure of the old regime—may have found a certain amount of material security in having a country estate and useful kinship relations, for this enabled him to be educated, and facilitated his passing the examinations and attaining a career in the service of the state. But it was only by being in office that he was able to make full use of his privileges, for then he no longer had to pay taxes and was exempted from corvée and, usually, from military service. The mere fact of being in office guaranteed to officials and their descendants the monopoly of education that provided such an inestimable source of prestige amidst a sea of illiterates. It also conferred special rights which in practice amounted to complete immunity before the law, in a country where the ordinary subject was deprived of all legal rights. . . . Moreover, official status allowed those who enjoyed it to enrich themselves by every means, legal or illegal, and to acquire new lands, or enlarge the family estate. The combination of these factors enabled the scholar-official gentry to continue in office and perpetuate themselves as the mandarinate that remained the ruling class until recent times.

Balazs shows, moreover, how the dominant class created and used the bureaucratic state for its own purposes, thereby stifling the forces and initiatives that otherwise would have tended to promote development. In traditional China the state had its finger in practically every pie. The trade in staples (salt was the most prominent) was organized as a system of monopolies with residual ownership vested in the state; merchants acquired the rights for particular regions from the state and ensured their trade by paying off regularly the officials responsible. The ownership of rental housing, shops, warehouses, and so forth, and urban real estate generally was divided between private individuals and the state. Foreign trade, like the domestic trade in staples, was the prerogative of the state, and the merchants who engaged in it, although accumulating among the largest merchant fortunes in China, did so as agents of the state. Because the leading merchants in both domestic and foreign trade were protected monopolists, they were not impelled to reinvest their profits in new enterprises or to protect their positions, and thus the fortunes that were accumulated did not serve to promote development.

The contribution of Balazs to our understanding of the forces that promoted underdevelopment in China, therefore, is a substantial one. His presentation does, however, have a number of defects, and I would like to turn to these next. They can be considered most conveniently under four distinct headings: (1) his understanding of class structure is not entirely correct; (2) his image of private forces as promoting development and the state as hindering it is overdrawn; (3) he does not consider sufficiently the impact of Western colonialism and imperialism; and, above all, (4) he fails to grasp the development of underdevelopment as a historical process. Why, for example, did not the bureaucratic state inhibit development during the Song dynasty as well as during the Qing dynasty? I would like to consider these criticisms in order.

Balazs talks of a distinct merchant class and a separate scholar-official class, and although he recognizes explicitly an "interpenetration" or "symbiosis" between the two, they remain in his view "two hostile but interdependent classes." As I show in my own account in the next section, however, by late imperial times there was in fact a single dominant elite class, the members of which sometimes served as officials, sometimes engaged in commerce or money-lending, sometimes derived substantial revenues from land-owning, and sometimes combined these activities. The difficulties China encountered in modernization in the late imperial period should be understood not as a consequence of the cooptation of a potentially progressive merchant class, but a consequence of a single dominant class firmly wedded to the existing order of which it was the principal and indeed sole beneficiary; this argument is spelled out in greater detail in the final section.

When Balazs (1972: 102) writes that "the bureaucracy was perfectly satisfied with traditional techniques," or sees the state bureaucracy as completely inimical to private initiative, he is clearly overstating a basically accurate perception. The overstatement, however, conceals a number of basic questions. In certain historical periods the bureaucracy did not suppress entrepreneurship—why? In the modernization process in other countries, the state has often taken a leading role; why was this not true in China? We simply cannot accept a unicausal theory of development based on private initiative or a theory which fails to recognize the positive potential of the state's role in development. Another weakness of Balazs's theory lies in his failure to recognize the part played by imperialism in China's failure to modernize, an impact which, as I have argued, although secondary, cannot be neglected entirely.

Perhaps the most important weakness in Balazs's theory is that it is simply not historical. Balazs does not make a distinction between periods of progress and periods of stagnation. He does not recognize the process of China's becoming underdeveloped as a historical process. The state is always evil, always a "totalitarian Moloch of a state" (p. 17). Essentially the same state, however, contributed to making China—or at least failed to hinder China from becoming—the world's most "advanced" nation until the Renaissance in the West. Balazs's theory, therefore, leaves us without an explanation of the historical forces bringing about the development of underdevelopment in China.

CLASS STRUCTURE AND THE
DEVELOPMENT OF UNDERDEVELOPMENT IN CHINA

In this section I would like to present my own understanding of the development of underdevelopment in China. To do so I believe it will be necessary first to clarify the class structure and relations of production that existed in late imperial China. Although my focus is on the nineteenth century, the structure with which I am concerned has, quite obviously, much deeper roots and I will try to indicate these where possible.

The class structure of late imperial China is marked by the common class identity of the various elite groups. Discussions of the merchant class, landlord class, government-official class, and of the gentry as an educated class tend to obscure this central fact by drawing the class lines in the wrong way. In fact, there was one dominant class, the gentry in late imperial China, drawing its income from the surplus produced by the peasants, artisans, and workers above their own subsistence requirements. Land-owning, money-lending, mercantile activity, official position and so forth were different means of garnering this surplus, not the demarcations of distinct classes.

Since the Song dynasty the gentry had enjoyed a substantial income from office and landownership. Income from business activity, always present in some measure, also became of great importance in the late imperial period. From about 1700, wealthy gentry families

> began to put more and more of their money into pawnbroking, so that control of rural credit was by the 19th century a major source of gentry wealth.

> Merchants and gentry had long been informally connected, and the division of urban society into mercantile and gentry spheres was already a fiction by the 18th century. Prominent lineages had members in both groups, and commercial pursuits were a surer road to gentry rank than simple land-holding [Wakeman, 1975a: 27, 234].

And gentry status, formally indicated by a degree received upon passing an examination or through purchase, was a prerequisite to holding office. Thus, although its members were engaged in different activities, there was one dominant class. This class was divided into two fairly distinct strata, one, rooted in the countryside, composed mainly of the lower gentry, and the other, distinguished by its large-scale activities and high income, composed of the upper gentry, officials, large merchants, large landowners, and so forth.

Officialdom was the principal path to fortune in imperial China. The average income of the 23,000 office holders in late nineteenth century China was more than 5,000 silver taels per year (Chang, 1962: 42; a tael is 1/16th of a catty or a little more than an ounce and in the 1880s was worth on the average U.S. $1.28). The average county magistrate (there were some 1,500 of them) received 30,000 taels per year, the average provincial governor 180,000 taels (Chang, 1962: 31-32). This compares to an average income of 10 taels per year for an average laborer (Chang, 1962: 101). To put these figures in perspective,[14] if an average laborer in the U.S. today earns $6,000, the average official received an amount comparable to $3 million annually, a magistrate $18 million, and a provincial governor $108 million—tax free of course. Of this income, only about one-nineteenth was salary; the rest came from unauthorized taxes and surtaxes, and from bribes (Chang, 1962: 10, 42).

> Of all the activities open to the gentry, the holding of office was not only the most distinguished career but was also almost the only way to amass a large fortune. In imperial Chinese society it was taken for granted that officeholding and wealth usually went together. There was a common saying: "May you be promoted in office and become rich."
>
> It was not only the high officials . . . who gained high income from office. We know from materials in local gazetteers and clan records that virtually all officials were able to acquire large sums. . . . An official career was regarded by the officials themselves and by all others as much more profitable than other occupations [Chang, 1962: 7-8].

The scale of official corruption thus was so huge that it not only afforded those concerned a life-style marked by extravagant luxury, it created as well enormous and concentrated pools of liquid capital for investment.

Some of this capital was used to acquire large land holdings. The net returns were some 5%-10% of the purchase price, about half of what alternative "investments"[15] could bring (Feuer-werker, 1976b: 82), but the status and security afforded by land-ownership and the self-satisfaction it afforded the owner made land a desirable purchase for men who could consume on a grand scale and engage in more lucrative investments at the same time. Thus Governor-General Li Hong-zhang's amassing of hundreds of thousands of acres of land and innumerable silk stores and pawnshops (Wakeman, 1975a: 193), while unusual in scale (this noted "reformer" was regarded by late nineteenth century contemporaries as the richest man in the world; Chang, 1962: 130), was not unusual in mixing official position with land-owning, mercantile interest, and money-lending.

Indeed, returns on land investment were too low to permit the amassing of large estates by the reinvestment of rental receipts and too low as well to assure the position of the commoner landlords, who were subject to the squeeze of local officials and their underlings. The escape from taxation of the powerful gentry households increased the pressure on the other land-owners. Moreover, in years of bad harvest, the full rent (normally half the crop) was difficult to collect. Under these circumstances, landowners of any size would seek the protection of gentry status, either by having their sons pursue the "regular" examina-tion route or by the purchase of a degree.[16] Thus, although not all members of the upper gentry had extensive land holdings, all large landowners tended to be members of the gentry. And smaller landowners too, wherever their resources permitted, also sought the protection and advantage of gentry status. About one-third of China's farmland was owned by landlords, and while precise quantification is difficult, it appears that about three-fourths of this was owned by members of the gentry (Chang,

1962: 144-145), who thus held about one-quarter of China's farmland.

Big business too was a gentry preserve, at least by the late imperial period. In the first place, the principal source of the substantial capital funds needed was official position, and in the second, official connections were of paramount importance in business success. The most profitable merchant activities, including especially the salt trade and foreign trade, were run as state-licensed monopolies. A substantial share of the profits were raked off by the officials charged with supervising these activities, and by the emperor and his family. Good official relations were necessary to secure and maintain the monopoly rights, and to keep the official rake-offs from assuming ruinous proportions.[17] In a society where the commoners could not ordinarily even gain audience with the officials, therefore, gentry status was essential for success in and maintenance of big business operations. It is not surprising then that "the records show that in the main the business administrators and the suppliers of capital in the salt trade were members of the gentry," and that despite the formal exclusion of gentry members from brokerage activities, "it was an open secret that hong merchants [foreign traders] were gentry" (Chang, 1962: 158, 165).

The ownership of financial enterprises was also almost exclusively in gentry hands. Here, in addition to securing protection from the most rapacious officials and acquiring the necessary rights, official connections were necessary to secure government deposits. In the pawnshops, Shanxi banks and native banks, the ability to deal with officials was of paramount importance, and the principal capital providers and managers were mainly gentry members.

The arrangements in the salt trade show how the interests of the officials (and the emperor in the most profitable businesses) and the gentry-merchants interpenetrated (Wakeman, 1975a: 49-50). The salt commissioner was typically an imperial household official who paid off his palace superiors to obtain his post. The emperor expected expensive presents from him, and if these were not forthcoming in sufficient magnitude could fine him heavily, or worse. His inducement to squeeze as much as possible was great, therefore, but it was tempered by his knowledge of the capital needs of the merchants, whose bankruptcy would halt the flow of salt revenue to the imperial household. These relations, which can perhaps best be expressed by the term "bureaucratic capitalism," reveal clearly the interdependence of the official and commercial interests. When industrial enterprises were initiated from the end of the nineteenth century, moreover, the major ones (limited in number) were almost exclusively the province of officials and those with close official connections. As Ho Ping-ti (1959: 206) states,

> Even in the late Ch'ing and early Republican period the few new industrial enterprises launched by the Chinese were almost invariably financed by bureaucratic capitalists. In the cotton textile industry, for example, out of a total of twenty-six mills established between 1890 and 1913, nine were established by active and retired high officials, ten by mixed groups of officials and individuals with official titles, and seven by the new breed of treaty-port compradores, practically all of whom had official connections. It is common knowledge that after the founding of the Nationalist government in 1927 a few top-ranking bureaucrats who enjoyed Chiang Kai-shek's confidence exerted ever more powerful control over the modern sector of the national economy through the incomparably superior apparatus of four major modern banks.

In rural China, the constellation of activities raking off the surplus in the late imperial period was much the same as in industry, except that the activities were carried out on a much smaller scale. The rural (usually lower) gentry tended to be made up of smaller landowners and moneylenders, lower retired officials, and so forth. Some engaged in mercantile activities, but in contrast to gentry-dominated big business, these were no more than a minute fraction of the innumerable petty traders and small businessmen of China; when they did engage in such activities, however, they enjoyed a distinct advantage over their commoner competitors.

Rural gentry were more likely to be engaged in activities like tax collection, teaching, the handling of legal affairs, and the management of semipublic activities. As tax farmers, they had an opportunity to profit handsomely from locally imposed surtaxes, which increased markedly over the course of the nineteenth century, often reaching several times the land tax remitted to the central government. Furthermore, as the local farmers paid their taxes in copper cash while the central government received the taxes in silver taels, the local gentry also stood to profit by manipulating the exchange rate between the two. Most of the local gentry served as teachers, averaging an income of about 100 taels, or as managers of public works projects, clan affairs, and so forth, in which capacity they received slightly more. Again comparison can be made with the 10-tael income of the average laborer, and it should be noted that such local gentry income was often combined with income from land-holding, money-lending, and so forth. At the start of the nineteenth century, 1.2% of the Chinese population were members of the gentry, and by the end of the century the proportion had risen to 1.9% (Chang, 1974: 140-141).

Above the direct producers in late imperial China, then, there was one elite class with two distinct strata skimming off the surplus which the peasants, artisans, and workers produced above their own subsistence requirements. The upper stratum was composed of high officials, big businessmen, and big landowners. The local stratum, much larger in number, dominated village life. The lowest level of central government authority in the countryside was the county magistrate, responsible in the nineteenth century for administering a district with typically some 250,000 people. This he could do only with the cooperation of the local gentry, thus inevitably involving them in tax-farming and other semiofficial activities. The local gentry role expanded still further during and after the Taiping Revolution, when the gentry took the leading role in organizing and maintaining the local militia. At both levels, therefore, there was a complete interpenetration of public office and private interest.

The maturing of bureaucratic capitalism in late imperial China was highly inimical to technological progress and economic development. The path to wealth was becoming or paying off an official, and neither new technology nor fixed capital was protected against official rapacity. The profitability of big business depended on monopoly and of all business on official connections. At the same time, the relations of production in both industry and agriculture, marked by the divorce of the merchants from productive activity and of the landlords from the land, further inhibited technological progress.

Mercantile profits were in distribution, and merchants tended to remain ignorant of the production processes for goods which they traded. The major wholesale cotton cloth dealers of Suzhou, for example, had nothing to do with production; they paid labor contractors a fixed price per piece rather than hire labor directly (Wakeman, 1975a: 42). Under these circumstances, the merchants remained largely ignorant of the techniques of production and were hardly in a position to improve them. In agriculture, the movement of substantial landowners to urban areas between the sixteenth and eighteenth centuries continued a process long under way and climaxed the demise of the estate system. Progressive, "improving" landlords who took an active interest in farm management and technique disappeared. Increasingly in the nineteenth century, landlord bursaries, often invested with police powers to arrest recalcitrant tenants, took over the task of rent collection for absentee landlords. Even where land-holdings were both substantial and geographically compact, the land was divided into small parcels and let out to separate tenants. The landowner, typically supplying no more than the land and sometimes the farm buildings, had nothing else to do with production and became a pure rentier. This pattern of production relations governed even the small landowners remaining in the countryside, and they too became purely parasitic.

Thus both in industry and agriculture, the production relations of late imperial China were marked by a fairly complete separation between large-scale owners and production processes. The path to profit was not the improvement of production but command over the social processes whereby the direct producers were relieved of the surplus they produced. The ruling class was the gentry class divided into two main strata, one composed of officials, large landowners, large moneylenders, and substantial merchants, the other, dominating the countryside, composed of smaller variants of these. Both levels carried out certain administrative and social operations necessary to keep Chinese society functioning. The system worked well from the standpoint of the gentry, providing them with wealth and status; there was no reason why they should want to change it, and indeed they did not want to do so.

The failure of China to experience substantive economic development (in a modern sense) prior to the twentieth century must be grasped in this context. The dominant gentry class was almost purely parasitic, marginally involved when involved at all in the processes of production. At the pinnacle of a society in which power, wealth, and education meant everything, they had everything. With the dominant class opposed to modernization or development and the threats to its position that social change would entail, it is natural that such change did not come readily.

To the extent that class structure accounts for the failure of China to develop economically in the late imperial period, the impediment posed by population expansion in the face of limited resources provides an inadequate explanation. Ascribing underdevelopment to population increase in the face of resource constraints, as Elvin (1973) and many others do, is a hopelessly unsatisfactory approach, confusing secondary factors with primary ones; it is somewhat like ascribing an automobile accident to a tree when a driver drives into one. As the misunderstanding about the role of population pressure is widespread, however, I believe it worthwhile to pause briefly here to place the population issue in the context I have just outlined. I do not wish to argue that population growth created no difficulties, but merely that the population growth rate was modest and that the central issue is why the moderate levels of capital formation and technological progress necessary to raise output more rapidly than this modest rate were not forthcoming.

The population of China increased from 270 million in 1770 to 410 million in 1850, and after a sharp fall brought by the Taiping Revolution increased again to 430 million in 1913 (Perkins, 1969: 16). These estimates are perforce crude ones, but they are satisfactory for revealing rough orders of magnitude. In the period of most rapid growth, 1770 to 1850, population grew at a rate of 0.5% per year. This is not a particularly rapid rate of growth and contrasts with rates in excess of 3% annually for many Third World countries today and a rate of 2.1% in China itself between 1953 and 1973 (Banister, 1977: 35). Some expansion in the cultivated area—which increased from about 950 million mu in 1770 to about 1,210 million mu in 1873 (Perkins, 1969: 16)—did take place as well as some capital formation in the form of water conservancy projects and so forth, so the rate of technological progress needed to assure growth in per capita output was indeed quite modest. Yet even this modest rate of progress—or the industrial capital formation that could in part have substituted for it—proved unattainable, not because the best innovations were "used up," but because the social and class structure discouraged the development of new ones.

The reasons for this I have already indicated; the elite class had little to do with actual production, and the path to riches was through connections and corruption rather than through innovation and capital formation. Moreover, the dominant Confucian ideology, precisely because it integrated the system and justified the exploitation at its core, could only discourage the scientific learning and outlook necessary to technical progress. The inhibition of innovation caused by China's socioeconomic structure is evident everywhere, but the following example, drawn from the sphere of China's international economic relations, is especially pertinent because it touches on the failure of China to borrow foreign technology as well as to develop its own.

The years between 1770 and 1850 was the period encompassing the industrial revolution in England, but there was no group in

China with an active interest in investigating and importing the new technology. This can only be understood in the context of a dominant class divorced from production and comfortable in the knowledge that, in the words of the Qian Long emperor, "we possess all things." Moreover, the restrictions on foreign trade, which reflected in part the monopoly-rake-off mentality of China's elite, also hindered the possibilities of technological borrowing.

This was shown clearly when a limited number of Chinese ports was opened to foreign trade betwen 1685 and 1760. Most of the trade was carried on by the English, and although they could buy at different ports, they often had to buy from one of the "king's merchants," monopolists who dominated several ports after buying a monopoly trading license from one of the emperor's sons (Wakeman, 1975a: 119-120). Guangzhou was the only city which could resist the monopolists, so more and more of the trade went there. The Cohong or foreign trade guild there, however, also held monopoly privileges, and its monopoly profits were in turn siphoned off to an extravagent extent to the "hoppo" or custom's officer. When an Englishman (James Flint) attempted to protest to the Qian Long emperor, the emperor responded by limiting all trade to Guangzhou, an edict which remained in effect from 1760 to 1833. The English traders did not realize that the hoppo was a member of the imperial household, and that the illicit income he received was being split with the emperor. Survival in the world of commerce for the members of the Cohong, then, as for Chinese in any profitable activity, depended on their official relations and had little or nothing to do with their knowledge of the conditions of production. Under such circumstances, innovation was hardly likely to be forthcoming.

The dominant Confucian ideology reinforced the social mechanisms inhibiting innovation. The entire hierarchical ordering of Chinese society was supported, justified, and indeed integrated by the social philosophy of subservience and status embodied in Confucian thought. As Balazs states (1972: 155):

After much hesitation, the officials adopted the Confucianist doctrine as being the ideology that best expressed their way of life, since, in spite of preaching respect for others, justice and reciprocity, these virtues were reserved for relations between educated people, whereas for the ordinary subject, the cardinal virtue was absolute obedience. Its unalterable aim was to maintain the status quo of the social hierarchy. Ancestor worship, divested of its earlier religious character, geared the social mechanism, regulating every detail of social relations. Respectfulness, humility, deference, docility, complete submission and subordination to elders and betters—these were the dominant features of the Confucian ethic that helped to cement the hierarchy, creating a patriarchal, paternalistic world in which gradations of rank, from the sovereign downward, were marked by the reciprocal relations of favor and obligation, and individual rights, initiative, and liberty were entirely lacking.

What is especially important to note here is that this ideology, so hostile to the development of free scientific inquiry, was consciously fostered "to maintain the status quo," to perpetuate a system of privilege.

Classical education was the proper, indeed only, education for elite status in Chinese society, and the examination system helped to insure the thorough inculcation of the values it embodied. Since classical education defined elite status and was completely integrated into the social structure, there was no space left for scientific or technical learning. The image of itself that Confucian ideology fostered in the gentry class was, moreover, inconsistent with the needs of modernization. As Wakeman (1975a: 31) observes, "Landholding suited the upper gentry's image of itself in retirement—benevolent gentlemen farmers composing poetry at their villa windows while loyal tenants toiled patiently in the distant fields." And Ho Ping-ti (1959: 205) points out that "Technological inventions were viewed as minor contrivances unworthy of the dignity of scholars." Moreover, since any effort to change the content of education threatened to make obsolete the learning to which the members of the elite had devoted much of their lives, and to make obsolete as well the whole system of status on which their positions depended, their committed resistance to educational reform until the very end of the nineteenth century can be readily understood. In this respect too the class structure of traditional Chinese society was inimical to economic development. It is to this structure, then, and to the relations of production associated with it rather than to population growth that we must look for an explanation of the development of underdevelopment in China.

To consider directly the causes of underdevelopment, some further clarification of its meaning is in order. There is no evidence to suggest that per capita national product in the nineteenth century was very different from that in Song China, and good reason to believe that it was not very different, especially as per capita agricultural product appears to have remained about the same, or at least to have shown no clear secular trend, between 1400 and the early twentieth century (Perkins, 1969: 14-15). The principal referent for underdevelopment then, in China as elsewhere, is not the decline over time in a country's per capita product, but its per capita product in relation to the rapidly growing per capita products of Western countries from the nineteenth century.

Underdevelopment, however, involves more than just a low production in relation to other countries; it would be improper, for example, to speak of Japan in the first half of the nineteenth century as underdeveloped despite a per capita product low in relation to that of England. Underdevelopment implies as well a relationship of inequality between the less developed country and more developed ones. This relationship is expressed in the following ways. First, the advanced country wields military and political power over the underdeveloped country, limiting the autonomy of the latter and placing its citizens in an inferior position. Second, the relationship between them tends to contribute to the growth of the advanced country but not to the development of the underdeveloped one. Third, and possibly most important, the relationship creates or strengthens classes in the underdeveloped country whose interest is more closely tied to the activities of the advanced country than to the development of their own country or to the welfare of their countrymen. Fourth, the underdeveloped country tends to be thrown into a state of financial, technological, and cultural dependency on the advanced countries. And fifth, disarticulation appears in the economy of the underdeveloped country in the sense that progress occurring in one sector of the economy does not readily stimulate changes elsewhere; key sectors of the economy are tied to developments abroad more closely than they are to other domestic sectors. Thus, insofar as the growth of the treaty ports stimulated a demand for imports rather than local manufacturing, or the movement of the gentry with their capital to the cities led ultimately to capital flight abroad rather than urban development, the Chinese economy manifested disarticulation.

In all of the respects enumerated, inequality in the relations between China and the West played an unmistakable role in the underdevelopment of China. But to recognize the importance of this relationship and to assign it primary causal responsibility are two different things. China became an underdeveloped country during the course of the nineteenth century as its economy remained traditional and it was forced into a subservient and dependent relationship by the West and Japan. To understand China's underdevelopment in this way, however, does not mean that the West and Japan took the leading role in creating underdevelopment. Rather, to determine the principal factor, it is necessary to address the more general question, why did economic development fail to take place in China?

Had economic progress continued prior to or during the industrial revolution in the West, China would not have become underdeveloped. And the principal barriers to economic progress in China were not foreign but domestic. The Chinese economy in late traditional times produced a substantial surplus above the subsistence needs of the population; why was not this surplus invested? The discussion above concerning class structure and relations of production has already, I believe, provided most of the answer. Yet the issue is of such central importance that I believe some further discussion of the size and mode of utilization of the surplus is in order.

In the agricultural sector, as I have noted above, the most readily quantifiable components of the surplus, expressed as a proportion of net domestic product in the 1930s—and nineteenth century figures would not have been very different—were 10.7% for land rent, 3.4% for farm business profits, 2.8% for interest payments, and 2.1% for taxes paid by owner-farmers, totaling in all 19.0% of the national income (Lippit, 1974: 76). These estimates are themselves based on conservative assumptions and exclude the graft payments to local officials and their underlings, special levies (including military exactions) and surtaxes, and the exactions of bandits, all of which properly form a part of the surplus. While these are not precisely quantifiable, we can estimate with a high degree of confidence that in the rural sector alone, at a very minimum, 25% of the national income (38% of the income generated in the rural sector, on the assumption that this amounted to 65% of the national income) represented a surplus above the subsistence needs of the population. In the urban sector, the profits generated by mercantile and banking activities, including the enormous monopoly profits in the salt trade and foreign trade, income from urban real estate, and the graft income of senior officials and the emperor cannot have accounted for less than an additional 5% of national income, so that the surplus in China as a whole cannot have been less than 30% of the national income. While Riskin (1975: 74) estimates an actual surplus of 27.2% for 1933, his estimates exclude the massive illicit payments that characterized Chinese society right through the Republican period, so his estimate is fully consistent with the 30% minimum estimated here. The point here is not to provide a precise estimate of the surplus, however, but merely to show that it was quite substantial, sufficient to have sustained a high rate of capital formation without depressing the living standards of the population.

Another way to examine the size of the surplus is through the estimates Chung-li Chang (1962) provides of the income of the gentry in late nineteenth century China and of the size of the national income. He estimates the gross national product (GNP) at 2,781 million taels (p. 296) but in relying on official data for the area of cultivated land understates the total by a fourth and income generated in the agricultural sector by a like amount (Feuerwerker, 1969: 2; Perkins, 1969: 16). Feuerwerker corects Chang's estimate accordingly to get an 1880's GNP of 3,339 million taels. This would correspond to a net national product of about 3,228 million taels, if depreciation was the same 3.3% share of gross product in the 1880s that it constituted in 1933 (Liu and Yeh, 1965: 68). Against this figure we can compare the income of the gentry, almost all of which represented surplus (although not all surplus income went to the gentry). Table 5 indicates gentry income by source.

According to the information provided in Table 5, the gentry which constituted 1.9% of the population, received 719 out of the 3,228 million taels of the net national product generated in the 1880s or some 22.3%. This figure, however does not include the

TABLE 5
Total Annual Gentry Income in the Late Nineteenth Century
According to Source (in millions of taels)

Service income		
Officeholding	121	
Gentry services	111	
Secretarial services	9	
Teaching	62	
Other services	9	
Total service income		312
Income from landholding		293
Income from mercantile activities		114
Total		719

SOURCE: Chung-li Chang (1962: 197).
NOTE: Chang estimates an income from land-holding of 220 million taels, based on the assumption that gentry landowners held one-fourth of the land under cultivation. However, since his estimate of the amount of land under cultivation is too low, I have adjusted upward the rental income by one-third in the same manner that the income generated in the agricultural sector was adjusted upward in calculating the GNP.

entire surplus; most notably it excludes the emperor's income, income from urban real estate, the income of nongentry land-lords, the profit income of rich peasants, the income from non-gentry money-lending, nongentry mercantile profits, and the incomes from graft and extortion of yamen underlings (who lacked both gentry and official status). If we approach estimates of the size of the surplus in this way, again it would appear that 30% of national income is the minimum conceivable level.

The uses of the surplus included primarily luxury consumption (including conspicuous consumption), the purchase of land, ceremonial expenditures, the military expenditures ncessary to defend the empire against the foreigners and against the Chinese, and expenditures on classical education (with a net social utility that may well have been negative). The direct exactions of imperialism did not amount to very much before the turn of the century and even then they never amounted to more than a very minor share of the total surplus. Capital flight, which also absorbed a share of the surplus in the twentieth century, was not important in the nineteenth. Given the class structure and production relations of late imperial Chinese society, there was little or no incentive to invest the surplus productively.

This class structure was not always the same. Between the decline of the aristocracy in the late Tang dynasty and the in-creasing consolidation of gentry authority during and after the late Song, space existed for innovative merchants and landlords, and in the context of the favorable exogenous conditions pro-vided by an expanding frontier, urban growth, and increasing domestic and foreign trade, these took a leading role in propelling forward China's medieval economic revolution. During the Song dynasty, merchants still existed as a class distinct from the scholar-officials, and in the countryside, rich peasants and improving landlords held a position unequalled before or since (McKnight, 1975: 99). Many of the estates were run, at least in part, as large-scale production units, and it was not unusual for landowners to be reading treatises on agriculture and seeking to improve cultivation. In the cities, official control over markets collapsed, prototype merchant and craft guilds arose, and a city bourgeoisie with its own new culture appeared (Shiba, 1975: 42). As later, it was wealth that mattered, but the road to wealth was not necessarily through corruption and monopoly, and at least some of the recipients of the economic surplus were concerned with improving production techniques and developing new or improved products. There is some evidence of renewed agricultural development in Ming times (Eberhard, 1971: 248-250) and the late-Ming/early-Qing period was marked by the rise of great merchants (Ho, 1959: 197-201), but the further development in the same period of absentee landlordship, continuing a long historical trend, and its functional equivalent in the parcelization of estates limited further agricultural development.

As for the great merchants, their behavior was not very different from that of their contemporary European counterparts in early capitalist development. From Dobb's description of the latter, the parallel is evident.

> One feature of this new mechant bourgeoisie that is at first as surprising as it is universal, is the readiness with which this class compromised with feudal society once its privileges had been won. The compromise was partly economic—it purchased land, entered into business partnerships with the aristocracy, and welcomed local gentry and their sons to membership of its leading gilds; it was partly social—the desire for inter-marriage and the acquisition of titles to gentility. . . . The degree to which merchant capital flourished in a country at this period affords us no measure of the ease and speed with which capitalist production was destined to develop: in many cases quite the contrary. . . . The needs that merchants and usurers served were largely those of lords and princes and kings. These new men had to be ingratiating as well as crafty; they had to temper extortion with fawning, combine avarice with flattery, and clothe a usurer's hardness in the vestments of chivalry. In the producer they had little interest save in his continuing submissiveness and for the system of production they had little regard save as a cheap and ready source of supply. . . . To acquire political privilege was their first ambition: their second was that as few as possible should enjoy it. Since they were essentially parasites on the old economic order . . . their fortune was in the last analysis associated with that of their host. By the end of the

> 16th century this new aristocracy . . . had become a conservative
> rather than a revolutionary force; and its influence was to retard
> rather than to accelerate the development of capitalism as a mode
> of production [Dobb, 1975: 121-122].

I have quoted Dobb at length because this striking parallel is of quite some importance in understanding the role of the Chinese merchants. The primary impetus for capitalist development in Europe came from producers accumulating capital, going into trade, and then reorganizing production free from guild restrictions (Marx, 1962: 318-331; Dobb, 1975: 123); the rise of great merchants, although it contributed to the growth of commodity production, did as much to forestall capitalist development as to further it. In the context of Chinese society, Confucian scruples were easily overcome in practice and successful merchants readily assimilated into the gentry class, becoming defenders of the status quo in much the same manner as their European counterparts. As for the rise of independent capitalist producers, there was simply no space for it in Chinese society. When the bureaucratic capitalist enterprises were nationalized in 1949, the enterprises owned by the "national bourgeoisie," smaller businessmen who had suffered like the peasants and workers from the joint domination of bureaucratic capitalism and imperialism, were left in private hands; in all they accounted for only 20% of the capital stock (Mao, 1974: 268), testimony to the weak position of competitive capitalism at the end of the Republican era.

·By the eighteenth century, absentee landlordism was the rule and gentry-merchant distinctions largely a fiction. There was no elite division to create a space where the forces of development— or the peasants and workers for that matter—could breathe. The examination system became totally irrelevant to the problems of society, with the candidates for office discouraged from discussing even current affairs from the late eighteenth century (Chang, 1974: 176). Corruption, always present, grew to reach extraordinary proportions in the nineteenth century. In 1727, the Yong Zheng emperor had ordered expansion of the purchase system (of the titles for gentry status) because he was aware of the extent of the corruption in the examination system (Chang, 1974: 115). In the nineteenth century, meddling in examinations by high officials to favor their relatives became common (Chang, 1974: 186) and by late Qing times, according to Feng Gui-fen, "Malpractices in examination [were] practiced by seven or eight out of ten men. Only one case in several years has been punished according to law" (Chang, 1974: 190).

The corruption existed at every level of Chinese society, permeating it to its core. Illegal surcharges which the gentry in their role as tax farmers imposed on the peasants reached as high as 250% in the nineteenth century while tax revenues reaching the government remained constant (Wakeman, 1975b: 15). Corruption had always been a way of life in China, but in the nineteenth century it reached unprecedented proportions, not to be exceeded until the first half of the twentieth century.

> Public office had always been a major source of private income in late imperial China. How much more so was private office, especially when it included such lucrative pursuits as arms-buying with accompanying salesmen's rebates, or railway building with accompanying contractors' kickbacks. Governor-General Li Hung-chang, for example, amassed hundreds of thousands of acres of land, innumerable silk stores, and pawnships across the empire. A common saying at the time alleged that "every dog that barks for Li is fat." . . . [T]he Chinese warships [in the Sino-Japanese War of 1894-1895] lacked explosive warheads for their naval shells because Li's purveyor, his son-in-law Chang P'ei-lun, had pocketed the money and bought hollow warheads from Krupp instead. Other associates had taken similar liberties. Torpedoes turned out to be filled with scrap iron instead of gunpowder and the munitions bags of Weihaiwei with sand instead of explosives [Wakeman, 1975a: 193].

The formula for early industrialization in China, *guandu shangban* (official supervision and merchant management), applied in companies organized under Li and those like him, extended the corruption and embezzlement of official and local Chinese life to the limited corporations of the industrial era.

The emperors of China had always been wary of allowing too much authority to devolve upon the local gentry. The Taiping Revolution in the middle of the nineteenth century, however, could only be defeated by allowing the local gentry to organize and head local militia, financed by special levies and surtaxes which they themselves administered. After 1864, local rebellions or unrest, foreign military pressure and the weakness of the central government forestalled the demobilization of the local militia that would otherwise have been in order (Wakeman, 1975a and 1975b). This was the situation out of which grew the warlordism that marked the first half of the twentieth century. Moreover, from being an extension of government in the countryside, the local gentry gradually became the government; there was no longer any check on the gentry's exploitation of the peasants. From collecting for their own pockets as much as two and one-half times the legal taxes in the nineteenth century, they came to collect as much as ten times in the twentieth century (Chen, 1973: 74). Local police often became private militia, and "as control fell almost entirely into the hands of the local elite, taxes and rents, public and private, fused together" (Wakeman, 1975b: 23).

The problem of the development of underdevelopment in China must be grasped in this context. Meaningful distinctions between officials and those involved in commerce and money-lending *as separate classes* disappeared, with landownership, public functions, and commercial activities common to both. The members of the elite in late traditional China enjoyed a status that combined power, prestige, wealth, and intellectual self-gratification, and derived tremendous satisfaction from their status. This elite truly felt itself to be an elite, and in the context of Chinese society, where personal relations are so important, the consciousness of elite status was constantly being reinforced through interaction with others. The intoxication of the elite with its own status is marvelously described in *The Scholars,* an eighteenth century novel by Wu Jing-zi. The following passage describes the impact on a scholar of 54, who after failing the examination more than 20 times, passed both the local and provincial examinations in succession.

Fan Chin feasted his eyes on this announcement, and, after reading it once to himself, read it once more aloud. Clapping his hands, he laughed and exclaimed, "Ha! Good! I have passed." Then, stepping back, he fell down in a dead faint. His mother hastily poured some boiled water between his lips, whereupon he recovered consciousness and struggled to his feet. Clapping his hands again, he let out a peal of laughter and shouted, "Aha! I've passed! I've passed!" Laughing wildly he ran outside, giving the heralds and the neighbors the fright of their lives. Not far from the front door he slipped and fell into a pond. When he clambered out, his hair was disheveled, his hands muddied, and his whole body dripping with slime. But nobody could stop him. Still clapping his hands and laughing, he headed straight for the market.

With the wealth brought by his new status, the protagonist moved into a new house. After several days, his mother admonished the maids to be careful with the dishes because they "don't belong to us."

"How can you say they don't belong to you madam?" they asked. "They are all yours."

"No, no, these aren't ours," she protested with a smile.

"Oh yes, they are," the maids cried. "Not only these things, but all of us servants and this house belong to you."

When the old lady heard this, she picked up the fine procelain and the cups and chopsticks inlaid with silver, and examined them carefully one by one. Then she went into a fit of laughter. "All mine!" she crowed. Screaming with laughter she fell backward, choked and lost consciousness [Wu, 1957: 65-77].

It was only natural that the beneficiaries of the traditional system would do everything in their power to preserve it.

Consider, for example, the elimination of corruption in government: that would have eliminated literally 95% of the income of government officials. Or consider the question of tax reform through the elimination of tax farming: that would have eliminated a major source of income for the local gentry. Among the most important of the reform issues, however, was that concerning the examination system, for the encouragement of scientific and technical studies was essential to Chinese development. But those who had invested the better part of their lives in a classical education, and increasingly those who had purchased degrees, were not about to see their investment in human capital —in themselves— made obsolete. They correctly perceived that their whole position would be undermined by the spread of technical learning.

The power of conservatism was shown most strongly during the Tongzhi reform movement of the 1860s. This was a time when China, having experienced two foreign invasions and a major revolutionary effort, might have been expected at last to begin taking determined steps in the direction of modernization. It was not prevented from doing so by the West, but by its own gentry class. While Mary Wright (1957: 312) is correct in saying that "The T'ung-chih [Tongzhi] Restoration failed because the requirements of a modern state proved to run directly counter to the requirements of the Confucian order," her statement might have been more to the point if she had added "and the class interest it represented."

A major step of the movement was the establishment of the Tongwen guan, a school to teach engineering, astronomy, and mathematics to students training for government service. Although the school survived various direct attacks in the 1860s it ultimately failed, in large measure because traditional learning remained the qualification for provincial office and the students neglected their Western studies to pursue traditional ones (Wright, 1957: 248). As Franke observes (1967a: 103), "In the 1860s the whole educated class in China still agreed that the traditional order should be preserved at all costs." The vast majority of the gentry members who violently opposed reform were convinced that change meant possible infringement on their own position and interests; they were of course correct, for the traditional order had an internal consistency that could not be preserved in a modern state.

The opposition to substantive reform came not only from the officials and the local gentry, but from the imperial rulers as well.

The attempt of the Ming dynasty officials to prohibit foreign trade altogether and the subsequent restrictions on it were in the interest more of imperial security than national security, and of imperial income rather than of national income. During the nineteenth century a similar policy prevailed with respect to industrial development. The imperial government believed—correctly—that industrial development, where it took place, would strengthen local authority vis-à-vis its own, and might, in the extreme case, pose a threat to the dynasty itself. Thus it was hesitant to support the schemes for industrial development advocated by the self-strengtheners. Here, the effort at self-preservation by the dominant element within the dominant class thwarted efforts at industrial development.

Thus in China there were no distinct elements within the elite to champion development. Rather, there was a strong consensus in favor of preserving the status quo. The impact of Western imperialism on Chinese development must be understood within this context of a single dominant class hostile to development. In one sense, underdevelopment in China was clearly a consequence of the outward thrust of the West: the military intrusion of the West, the dependency and economic disarticulation that accompanied it, and the inequality manifest in extraterritoriality, loss of tariff control, and so forth, are indeed constitutent elements in underdevelopment. In a more basic sense, however, China set itself up as a victim for Western aggression when its own elite class successfully thwarted the forces of development. As Mao Ze-dong stated in 1937,

> The fundamental cause of the development of a thing is not external but internal. . . . The contradictions within a thing are the fundamental cause of its development, while its interrelations with other things are secondary causes. [Mao, 1968: 26; I have corrected the translation slightly to make the English read more smoothly.]

As I have indicated, the direct impact on China of Western colonial-imperialist activity was mixed. The treaty ports were sources of new technology, centers for investment, facilitators of the development of Chinese as well as of foreign enterprises, and were sources of moderate stimuli through linkage relations with the rest of the Chinese economy, to cite several of the favorable impacts. On the other hand, the Western intrusion forced opium on China, prevented a rational trade policy, damaged some handicraft industries, and diverted resources to defense and later to indemnities, among other negative impacts. These direct impacts are secondary, however. China became an under-developed country in the late imperial era because the interest of the gentry class was in preserving the status quo, because the economic and social changes associated with economic develop-ment would have undermined the social order that provided everything it wanted. And China remained an underdeveloped country in the first half of the twentieth century because the class structure and relations of production remained largely un-changed. As Balazs (1972: 117) states:

> The nationalist bourgeoisie of the Kuomintang equaled the offi-cials of the Celestial Empire in corruption, nepotism, bureaucracy, and inefficiency, and it was only to be expected that this national-socialist police state should firmly restore Confucianism and inscribe the ancient Confucian virtues upon its flag.

In the countryside of Republican China power remained in the hands of warlords and an ever-more corrupt gentry, while the bureaucratic capitalism used to pursue industrial development was merely a variant of the traditional use of state power to pursue private ends. Although the bourgeoisie of the Republican era cannot be said to have had a class interest actively hostile to economic development in the same sense as the imperial gentry had, their corruption and inefficiency, holdovers of the tradi-tional order, continued to forestall it. Without denying the significance of its antecedents, unambiguous progress toward economic development in China began with the success of the revolution in 1949, when the class of direct producers, of workers and peasants, a class with an undiluted interested in economic development, gained authority.

I have tried to argue here that while the concept of underdevelopment derives from the development and aggressive outward thrust of the West, the weakness of the Chinese response to this thrust and China's victimization by it reflect primarily the opposition to modernization by the dominant gentry class, which was the beneficiary of the status quo. This was a class that developed over the centuries by incorporating within itself all of the separate groups that lived off the surplus created by the direct producers. Even as it did so, eradicating the distinctions among the groups, it became more and more detached from production itself. In this sense, the development of underdevelopment in China is more properly attributable to the domestic class structure and relations of production than to external influence. As a consequence of both of its objective interest and its self-image, the gentry class was committed to preserving the existing order. The development of underdevelopment of China, then should be understood in terms of the emergence of a constellation of domestic forces inhibiting progress, into which constellation a rapacious West intruded.

NOTES

1. This passage is from Wu Zi-mu, *Meng-liang Lu* (Account of the Gruel Dream), preface dated September 16, 1274. This book is the most importance source of information regarding Hangzhou at the end of the thirteenth century, and is extensively discussed in Balazs (1972: 82-100).

2. Elvin also cites a change in the attitude of philosphers toward nature, but it seems more appropriate to regard this as a consequence rather than as a cause of economic decline.

3. Elvin (1973: 248-249) suggests that elite income from land-holding became relatively unimportant compared to other income sources in the late imperial period, but the impression he conveys is misleading. See the following discussion in the text and the quantitative estimates in the final section of this article.

4. As later discussion shows, practically all of the principal landowners had gentry status, and members of the gentry class owned about three-fourths of the land that was rented out.

5. On this issue see Myers (1970 and 1977), Hou (1965), Murphy (1974), and Esherick (1972). The first three of these authors argue that imperialism did little damage to the Chinese peasants; Esherick strongly objects.

6. Although the Taiping Revolution is usually referred to as the Taiping Rebellion, the usual term is clearly a misnomer, for this movement, seeking the transformation of society, clearly had both organization and ideology. I have therefore used the term "revolution" whenever I refer to it.

7. The population of Manchuria, including foreigners, increased from 9 million in 1895-1900 to 20 million in 1916 and 31 million in 1930-1931 (Sun, 1969: 21).

8. The aggregate impact of this expansion, however, remained slight because the amount of modern industry to begin with was miniscule.

9. For incisive critiques of the misuse of stage theories in economic development see Baran and Hobsbawn (1973), and Griffin (1973).

10. A paradigm in any discipline provides the intellectual framework within which it is grasped, determines the types of research investigations that will be undertaken, and provides criteria for assessing the validity of research methods. Probably the best guide to the emerging radical paradigm is provided by the collection of essays in Wilber (1973).

11. For an in-depth historical study showing how Western contact took the leading role in creating underdevelopment in Chile and Brazil, see Frank (1967).

12. Among those who take the contrary view that the foreigner was a necessary agent in China's modernization are Dernberger (1975), Eckstein and Fairbank (1975). This contrary view is presented in the most extreme form by Elvin (1973: 315), who writes, "It was the historic contribution of the modern West to ease and then break the high-level equilibrium trap in China."

13. For an account of the Taiping Revolution and of the Taiping program and objectives, see Shih (1967) and Franke (1976b). Despite the title of his essay—"The Taiping Rebellion"—Franke too regards the movement as a revolution rather than as a rebellion.

14. This is especially desirable because of the widespread fiction created in the literature that income differentials were not very great in traditional China (see, for example, Murphy, 1974: 46).

15. I am using the term "investment" here in the colloquial sense rather than in the economist's sense of capital formation.

16. Other measures included a suitably arranged marriage, the adoption of a promising scholar, and false registration.

17. Polachek (1975: 211-213) tells the story of a wealthy moneylender who in 1854 advanced a loan secured by a stolen official stamp. The local magistrate saw the opportunity to raise funds for the local militia and fined him 10,000 taels. The outraged moneylender sought the protection of the noted reformer Feng Gui-fen, who promised to fix his case if he would give 2,500 taels to Feng's relatives to endow a public mortuary. This case demonstrates the arbitrariness of the fines levied, the lack of legal recourse of citizens, and the importance of relations with (and pay-offs to) officials for self-protection.

REFERENCES

BALAZS, ETIENNE (1972) Chinese Civilization and Bureaucracy. New Haven: Yale Univ. Press.

BANISTER, JUDITH (1977) "China's demographic transition in the Asian Context," from "The current vital rates and population size of the People's Republic of China and its provinces." Ph.D. dissertation, Food Research Institute, Stanford University. Presented at the Conference on the Modern Chinese Economy in a Comparative Context, Stanford University, January 8.

BARAN, PAUL (1968) The Political Economy of Growth. New York: Monthly Review.

—— and E. J. HOBSBAWM (1973) "The stages of economic growth: a review," in C. K. Wilber (ed.) The Political Economy of Development and Underdevelopment. New York: Random House.

BARNETT, ROBERT (1941) Economic Shanghai. New York: Institute of Pacific Relations.

BUCK, JOHN L. (1968) Land Utilization in China. New York: Paragon Book Reprint.

CHANG, CHUNG-LI (1974) The Chinese Gentry. Seattle: Univ. of Washington Press.

—— (1962) The Income of the Chinese Gentry. Seattle: Univ. of Washington Press.

CHANG, JOHN K. (1969) Industrial Development in Pre-Communist China. Chicago: Aldine.

CHEN HAN-SENG (1973) Landlord and Peasant in China. Westport, CT: Hyperion Press.

CHESNEAUX, JEAN, MARIANNE BASTID, and MARIE-CLAIRE BERGERE (1976) China from the Opium Wars to the 1911 Revolution. New York: Pantheon.

DENNERLINE, J. (1975) "Fiscal reform and local control: the gentry-bureaucratic alliance survives the conquest," in F. Wakeman (ed.) Conflict and Control in Late Imperial China. Berkeley: Univ. of California Press.

DERNBERGER, R. (1975) "The role of the foreigner in China's economic development, 1840-1949," in D. Perkins (ed.) China's Modern Economy in Historical Perspective. Stanford: Stanford Univ. Press.

DOBB, MAURICE (1975) Studies in the Development of Capitalism. New York: International Publishers.

EBERHARD, WOLFRAM, (1971) A History of China. Berkeley: Univ. of California Press.

—— (1962) Social Mobility in Traditional China. Leiden: E. J. Brill.

ECKSTEIN, A., J. K. FAIRBANK, and L. S. YANG (1975) "Economic change in early modern China," in A. Eckstein, China's Economic Development. Ann Arbor: Univ. of Michigan Press.

ELVIN, MARK (1973) The Pattern of the Chinese Past. Stanford: Stanford Univ. Press.

ESHERICK, J. (1972) "Harvard on China: the apologetics of imperialism." Bull. of Concerned Asian Scholars 4, 4 (December 1972).

FAIRBANK, JOHN K. (1971) The United States and China. Cambridge, MA: Harvard Univ. Press.

—— and EDWIN O. REISCHAUER (1960) East Asia: The Great Tradition. Boston: Houghton Mifflin.

FEI, HSIAO-TUNG (1968) China's Gentry. Chicago: Univ. of Chicago Press.

——— (1945) Earthbound China: A Study of Rural Economy in Yunan. Chicago: Univ. of Chicago Press.

FEUERWERKER, ALBERT (1976a) The Foreign Establishment in China in the Early Twentieth Century. Ann Arbor: Univ. of Michigan Center for Chinese Studies.

——— (1976b) State and Society in Eighteenth-Century China: The Ch'ing Empire in Its Glory. Ann Arbor: Univ. of Michigan Center for Chinese Studies.

——— (1975) Rebellion in Nineteenth-Century China. Ann Arbor: Univ. of Michigan Center for Chinese Studies.

——— (1969) The Chinese Economy, ca. 1870-1911. Ann Arbor: Univ. of Michigan Center for Chinese Studies.

FRANK, ANDRE GUNDER (1973) "The development of underdevelopment," in C. K. Wilber (ed.) The Political Economy of Development and Underdevelopment. New York: Random House.

——— (1967) Capitalism and Underdevelopment in Latin America. New York: Monthly Review.

FRANKE, WOLFGANG (1967a) China and the West: The Cultural Encounter, 13th to 20th Centuries. New York: Harper.

——— (1976b) "The Taiping rebellion," in F. Schurmann and O. Schell (ed.) Imperial China. New York: Vintage.

FURTADO, C. (1973) "The concept of external dependence in the study of underdevelopment," in C. K. Wilber (ed.) The Political Economy of Development and Underdevelopment. New York: Random House.

GERNET, JACQUES (1970) Daily Life in China on the Eve of the Mongol Invasion, 1250-1276. Stanford: Stanford Univ. Press.

GRIFFIN, K. (1973) "Underdevelopment in history," in C. K. Wilber (ed.) The Political Economy of Development and Underdevelopment. New York: Random House.

HAEGER, J. (1975) "Introduction," in J. W. Haeger (ed.) Crisis and Prosperity in Sung China. Tucson: Univ. of Arizona Press.

HINTON, WILLIAM (1966) Fanshen. New York: Monthly Review.

HO, PING-TI (1962) The Ladder of Success in Imperial China. New York: Columbia Univ. Press.

——— (1959) Studies on the Population of China, 1386-1953. Cambridge, MA: Harvard Univ. Press.

HOU, CHI-MING (1965) Foreign Investment and Economic Development in China. Cambridge, MA: Harvard Univ. Press.

KIYOKAWA YUKIHIKO (1975) "Ideorogi to shite no gijyutsu to keizai hatten" (Technology as ideology and economic development: an analysis of the political economy of technology transfer). Ajia keizai 16, 4 (April 15, 1975).

LEVY, MARION (1949) The Family Revolution in Modern China. Cambridge, MA: Harvard Univ. Press.

LIPPIT, VICTOR D. (1974) Land Reform and Economic Development in China: A Study of Institutional Change and Development Finance. White Plains NY: International Arts & Sciences Press.

LIU, TA-CHING and KUNG-CHIA YEH (1965) The Economy of the Chinese Mainland: National Income and Economic Development, 1933-1959. Princeton: Princeton Univ. Press.

McKNIGHT, B. E. (1975) "Fiscal privileges and the social order in Sung China," in J. W. Haeger (ed.) Crisis and Prosperity in Sung China. Tuscon: Univ. of Arizona Press.

MAO ZE-DONG [Mao Tse-tung] (1974) Miscellany of Mao Tse-tung Thought (1949-1968) Part II. Springfield, VA: National Technical Information Service, U.S. Department of Commerce.

——— (1968) "On contradiction," in Four Essays on Philosophy. Beijing: Foreign Languages Press.

——— (1960) Analysis of the Classes in Chinese Society. Beijing: Foreign Languages Press.

MARX, KARL (1962) Capital, Volume III. Moscow: Foreign Languages Publishing House.

MULLER, R. (1973) "The multinational corporation and the underdevelopment of the third world," in C. K. Wilber (ed.) The Political Economy of Development and Underdevelopment. New York: Random House.

MURPHY, R. (1974) "The treaty ports and China's modernization," in M. Elvin and G. W. Skinner (eds.) The Chinese City Between Two Worlds. Stanford: Stanford Univ. Press.

MYERS, RAMON (1977) "Trends in agriculture: 1911-1949." Delivered at the Asian Studies on the Pacific Coast 1977 Conference, Eugene, Oregon, June 18.

——— (1970) The Chinese Peasant Economy: Agricultural Development in Hopei and Shantung, 1890-1949. Cambridge, MA: Harvard Univ. Press.

MYRDAL, JAN (1965) Report from a Chinese Village. New York: Pantheon.

NURKSE, RAGNAR (1964) Problems of Capital Formation in Underdeveloped Countries. New York: Oxford Univ. Press.

PERKINS, D. (1975) "Growth and changing structure of China's twentieth-century economy," in D. Perkins (ed.) China's Modern Economy in Historical Perspective. Stanford: Stanford Univ. Press.

——— (1969) Agricultural Development in China 1368-1968. Cambridge, MA: Harvard Univ. Press.

POLACHEK, J. (1975) "Gentry hegemony: Soochow in the T'ung-chih restoration," in F. Wakeman (ed.) Conflict and Control in Late Imperial China. Berkeley: Univ. of California Press.

RISKIN, C. (1975) "Surplus and stagnation in modern China," in D. Perkins (ed.) China's Modern Economy in Historical Perspective. Stanford: Stanford Univ. Press.

SCHULTZ, THEODORE (1964) Transforming Traditional Agriculture. New Haven: Yale Univ. Press.

SCHURMANN, FRANZ and O. SCHELL [eds.] (1967) Imperial China. New York: Vintage.

SEERS, D. (1973) "The meaning of development," in C. K. Wilber (ed.) The Political Economy of Development and Underdevelopment. New York: Random House.

SELDEN, MARK (1972) The Yenan Way in Revolutionary China. Cambridge, MA: Harvard Univ. Press.

SHIBA, Y. (1975) "Urbanization and the development of markets in the lower Yangtze valley," in J. Haeger (ed.) Crisis and Prosperity in Sung China. Tucson: Univ. of Arizona Press.

——— (1970) Commerce and Society in Sung China. Ann Arbor: Univ. of Michigan Center for Chinese Studies.

SHIH, VINCENT (1967) The Taiping Ideology. Seattle: Univ. of Washington Press.

SPENCE, JONATHAN D. (1975) "Opium smoking in Ch'ing China," in F. Wakeman (ed.) Conflict and Control in Late Imperial China. Berkeley: Univ. of California Press.

——— (1974) Emperor of China: Self-Portrait of K'ang-hsi. New York: Alfred A. Knopf.

SUN, KUNGTU C. (1969) The Economic Development of Manchuria in the First Half of the Twentieth Century. Cambridge, MA: Harvard Univ. Press.

WAKEMAN, FREDERIC E., Jr. (1975a) The Fall of Imperial China. New York: Free Press.

——— (1975b) "The evolution of local control in late imperial China," in F. Wakeman (ed.) Conflict and Control in Late Imperial China. Berkeley: Univ. of California Press.

——— (1966) Strangers at the Gate: Social Disorder in South China 1839-1861. Berkeley: Univ. of California Press.

WILBER, CHARLES K. [ed.] (1973) The Political Economy of Development and Underdevelopment. New York: Random House.

WRIGHT, MARY C. (1957) The Last Stand of Chinese Conservatism: Stanford: Stanford Univ. Press.

WU JING-ZI [WU CHING-TZU] (1957) The Scholars. Beijing: Foreign Languages Press.

YANG, C. K. (1965) Chinese Communist Society: The Family and the Village. Cambridge, MA: MIT Press.

Victor D. Lippit is Associate Professor of Economics at the University of California, Riverside. He is the author of Land Reform and Economic Development in China: A Study of Institutional Change and Development Finance. *This study is the first section of his new book,* The Economic Development of China, *to be published by M. E. Sharpe.*

Comment

MARK ELVIN

University of Oxford

There is an unavowed and very questionable premise underlying "surplus theories" of economic history such as Professor Lippit's. This is the implied assumption that the leisure preference of the labor force is zero. Alternatively, it amounts to saying that the imposition of rents and taxes that lower a worker's wages never induce any effort on his (or her) part to work harder or longer in order to recover some of the lost income.

A formal representation can be given in the terms made familiar by Chayanov's theory of the peasant economy. It is shown here as Figure 1, under the provocative title of "Exploitation as a Cause of Increased Production." Chayanov argued that the peasant characteristically worked until he reached some sort of an equilibrium at which the output to be gained from further exertions was not judged to be a reasonable exchange for the irksomeness of the extra effort required. In a social system free of rents and taxes, this point may be thought of as the E_f of the diagram. If we now extend Chayanov's scheme and imagine that the system has become an exploitative one, with the landlord's rent of size S_1, the wages of the peasant will fail to W'_e if he makes no effort to resist the decline.

Most economic historians would, I believe, accept it as more likely that in most situations the peasant (or other worker) will labor longer or harder to increase his output to $O_e > O_f$, so that while he still loses S_1 to the landlord (or other boss), he takes home W_e, less than his wages under freedom but more than W'_e.

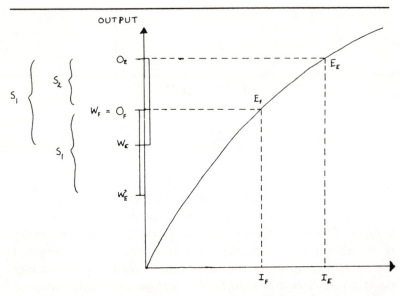

IRKSOMENESS OF LABOR

NOTE: Explanation of symbols: I_f and I_e = irksomeness of labor under a free and exploitative system, respectively. O_f and O_e = output under a free and exploitative system, respectively, with W_f and W_e the corresponding wages actually received. W'_e = wages that would accrue given output O_f and a rent or comparable deduction of size S_1, made by a landlord or other exploiter. S_2 = surplus production created in response to landlord's exactions.

Figure 1: Exploitation as a Cause of Increased Production

In other words, the pressure of exploitation has created output to the value of S_2 that would *otherwise never have existed.* In contrast, the surplus theory historian implicitly denies that E_e and E_f are distinct, or at least that it can ever be the case that $O_e > O_f$, since it is sometimes hinted that $O_f > O_e$.

Until solid evidence is provided to justify this denial, or convincing measures are found for S_2 as well as the familiar S_1, all attempts to quantify amounts of "surplus" are bogus, since an undefined proportion would vanish if the exploiters disappeared.

Mark Elvin is University Lecturer in Chinese History at the University of Oxford, and a Fellow of St. Anthony's College, Oxford. His chief interests are economic history and premodern demography.

A White Horse May or May Not Be a Horse, but Megahistory Is Not Economic History

ALBERT FEUERWERKER

University of Michigan

To put it directly, in the last section of his essay where Professor Lippit offers his "own understanding of the development of underdevelopment" in China, the author—with the innocence of a first kiss—discovers the gentry and Confucianism. Possibly there are yet some students of modern China to whom it is a novel proposition that the interests of the mainstream of the gentry and the Confucian ideology which protected them were inimical to modern economic development. It is difficult to believe, however, that the weight of that useful proposition is increased merely—and this is all that Lippit adds for his innocent readers—by the wisdom implicit in the words "class" and "relations of production." Except for those incredibly isolated from useful books, these sobriquets can hardly arouse now any sense of new discovery.

Lippit's major criticism of the various theories of underdevelopment, which he considers in the third section of his work before offering his own discovery in the fourth section, is that they are ahistorical, that they do not confront the question of how underdevelopment develops. He encounters, however, both conceptual and—as I shall indicate below—substantive difficulties with the task of showing that underdevelopment was an en-

81

dogenous process experienced by the Chinese economy. Having acknowledged that total output expanded and that there is no evidence of any decline in per capita national product between 1400 and the early twentieth century, Lippit proceeds to define underdevelopment in relative terms. "The principal referent for underdevelopment then, in China as elsewhere, is not the decline over time in a country's per capita product, but its per capita product in relation to the rapidly growing per capita products of Western countries from the nineteenth century." But such a "principal referent" only carries meaning "elsewhere" when it can at least be postulated that the growth of the advanced countries has been significantly furthered by their economic exploitation of the less developed ones.

There would immediately have been a further problem if the author had here opted for a paradigm of underdevelopment possibly applicable to relatively small Latin American and Southeast Asian nations, which became heavily dependent on international markets, and attempted to lay the continental mass of China on that Procustean bed. But he avoids such a misstep and correctly concludes that the economic consequences of imperialism in China were ambiguous. (Imperialism—I have argued this elsewhere—had powerful effects in China's modern history, but undermining the premodern economy was not one of them.) He does resort to a hurried passage, curiously abstract, about the role of "inequality in the relations between China and the West . . . in the underdevelopment of China." Since the effects of the foreign economic presence have already been discounted, this "does not mean that the West and Japan took the leading role in creating underdevelopment." Lippit is thus aware of the difficulty of applying the trendy notion "development of underdevelopment" to China once the onus of imperialism has been lightened. He retains, however, enough of a commitment to the concept, whatever the facts for China, for him to borrow Andre Gunder Frank's title and to propose to answer with a single domestic factor the question of why the Chinese economy "developed" from being highly developed (in the Song dynasty, for example) to underdevelopment (in the nineteenth and twentieth centuries).

Only he accomplishes nothing of the sort. The fourth section is no more than a static description of the late-Qing gentry in their economic, social, and political roles. The evolution of the Chinese economy from the Song to the Qing is relegated to a few pages (in the first and second sections and a few hints elsewhere) which are as barren of real economic history as this reader has ever seen for paragraphs appearing under such a title as "A Thumbnail Sketch of Chinese Economic History Since 960."

If there is a developmental process suggested at all, it is limited to the almost offhand proposal that the post-Song gentry increasingly incorporated the merchant stratum which during the Song dynasty "still existed as a class distinct from the scholar-officials." The gentry class "developed over the centuries by incorporating within itself all of the separate groups that lived off the surplus created by the direct producers." Perhaps. But Lippit shows no apparent awareness of the by now quite immense literature in Chinese, Japanese, and Western languages which might either support or contradict his suggestion. And, unfortunately, for the nineteenth century—when underdevelopment mainly "developed" —and later, the dominant process with respect to the gentry was quite the opposite of what he proposes. From midcentury onward and with increasing impetus we can discern a differentiation of the gentry, as its sons (and occasionally daughters) took on the roles of import-export merchants, manufacturers, bankers, "modern" intellectuals (teachers, students, journalists, doctors, lawyers, engineers), politicians (reformist bureaucrats, constitutionalists, revolutionaries), and new-style military officers. The main body, the majority, of the gentry retained its conservative attitude—toward economic change and much else. But it was these new social strata who were the dynamic actors at the end of the dynasty and the beginning of the republic, and they were no longer crudely opposed to economic development (or even to social change within limits) on the grounds that it might threaten their class interests. It is simply untrue that the probable reinforcement of the power of the lower rural gentry by the centrifugal results of the 1911 revolution was the major reason—it was of course one factor among others—for China's underdevelopment in the twentieth century.

As will now be apparent, what troubles me about this essay is not any serious disagreement with its principal theme, namely, that the class and social structure of Qing China inhibited modern economic growth, while some of the rest of the world (Europe, the United States, Japan) proceeded varying distances along the development road, with the result that China which ranked as a leader, or at least an equal, prior to the Industrial Revolution, and so on, was dumped into the cellar of underdevelopment. What does trouble me—and should discomfort anyone who believes in the value of a deep and genuine understanding of the Chinese experience past and present—is the enormous distance that exists between Professor Lippit's megahistorical approach and the need to come to grips with the complex dynamics of China's economy and society. Sustained consideration of the historical evidence on any economic issue or any event with possibly large implications for the economy is usurped by polemics (admittedly quite mild), random anecdotal history (such as historians themselves seldom perpetrate any more), and the wide-eyed discovery of what is already widely known. Take, for example, the "Thumbnail Sketch" to which I have already referred. It is nearly unbelievable that these pages do not even attempt to summarize the changes that occurred over 900 years in the principal magnitudes and institutions that are the subjects of economic history: output and its sectoral origin, income per capita and its distribution, population and its employment, land and its utilization, capital and its composition (including technology), money and its quantity and circulation, kinds and quantities of "social overhead capital" and services, government revenue and expenditure, economic theory and policy, and so forth. The remarkable economic expansion of the late seventeenth and eighteenth centuries—about which we now know a great deal even if still not enough, and which would seem to offer the possibility for valuable insights into subsequent stagnation—is passed by in a few lines completely lacking in analytic content.

Precisely this same innocence about China's real economic history informs Lippit's critique of various theories of underdevelopment in the third section. He does indeed make some useful sallies against those who might wish to rely exclusively on any of these six explanations of China's economic backwardness in their most general forms. But the issue of "wrong" or "right" at the level of abstraction at which Lippit remains, although it may have its aficionados, is not the one that should properly occupy the principal attention of any student who desires to go beyond caricaturing Chinese economic history. The experience of one-quarter of the human race—if only for its mass—merits genuine historical analysis which penetrates beneath its notorious physiognomy (even the most accurate caricature provides no more) to a systematic, analytic, comparative study of its real anatomy and physiology. What I mean, of course, is that all six of the theories pummeled by Lippit are "wrong" in the sense that accepting any of them as an adequate statement precludes genuine knowledge (which also requires detail and idiosyncracy) because each is so general that it obscures or abandons the valuable insights—at some level of analysis—proffered by the others. But if we accept with equal finality the "theory" offered by Lippit in the fourth section, and rest content with his generalities, we commit the same fault a seventh time. What is challenging in the study of China's economic history is not merely to label the class and social structure of Qing China as obstructive to development, but to demonstrate with as high a degree of verisimilitude as possible the complex processes and institutions by means of which the Confucian elite maintained itself, produced and distributed society's goods and services, and fended off economic and social change.

These are genuine historical problems of the highest order of intellectual importance and moral relevance. But their pursuit requires more than a justifiable sense of outrage at China's fate—and less justly at those scholars who are too ignorant or too misguided to understand simplified Marxism. To outrage must be added useful theory and intimate acquaintance with the prodigious historical sources. The several theories of underdevelopment discussed in the third section, impotent as each is to explain all, do however in some cases suggest the intervening mechanisms (organisms? systems?) by means of which our Confucian elite built and sustained their kind of society for so long. It is through the analysis of such relationships, institutions, and processes at the middle range and lower that we shall be able to link theory and empirical data to achieve a more adequate understanding of China's economic and social history.

I doubt, for example, that "Preindustrial Stage Theory" (which derives from Professor Rostow's "stages of economic growth") was ever a very valuable analytic tool. But it does have the virtue, which Lippit's essay lacks, of acknowledging a distinction between premodern and modern economic growth. There is—I would argue, and Lippit of course disagrees: "the rate of technological progress needed to assure growth in per capita product was indeed quite modest," he asserts without evidence—a qualitative difference between slow and fluctuating growth of output, and so on within a slowly changing ("traditional") technology such as China experienced over the centuries and "modern economic growth" (under capitalism or socialism) as defined by Professor Kuznets. Those conditions which conduced to premodern economic growth from the Song to the Qing may have been precisely the principal obstacles to modern economic development. Thus from the point of view of "modern economic growth," a process which Lippit himself certainly agrees has occurred in China since 1949, "underdevelopment" *is* a characteristic of all "traditional societies." Indeed it may be the "normal" state of things on the scale of world history, so that the really significant intellectual task is to account for the rapid development of the West and Japan.

The "Vicious Circle of Poverty Thesis" as an explanation of China's underdevelopment errs as Professor Lippit points out in greatly underestimating the savings potential—i.e., the surplus above subsistence requirements—of the Chinese economy. Although a surplus in this sense must exist in general for the social system to continue along its traditional path, it is nevertheless possible—indeed inevitable—that at specific times and in definite places both the supply of savings and the demand for investment were inadequate for the purposes of sustaining or increasing output. While conceptually a surplus always exists, in real history the choices, frictions, and accidents of man producing and consuming in a complex society may make Nurske's formulations quite useful tools for detailed historical analysis of real cases. Take, for example, Professor Lippit's estimate of the actual rural surplus in 1933 as equal to 19% of net domestic product. He assumes that after deducting the proportion of investment, communal services, and government consumption attributable to the rural surplus (4% out of a total of 5.8% of NDP for these purposes in 1933), 15% of NDP was utilized for luxury consumption by the rural elite, but might potentially have been available for productive investment. Indeed some part of the rural surplus was wasted in luxury consumption, but other parts were hoarded, "invested" in real estate, or reloaned to peasant borrowers. The principal difficulty with assuming a rural surplus above mass consumption equivalent to 15% of NDP available for redistribution in 1933 is that neither Lippit nor I have any useful quantitative data with which to estimate the importance of these various alternative uses of the surplus. If, for example, net landlord purchases of agricultural land and urban real estate, hoarding of gold and silver, and consumption loans to farmers were large, this in effect involved a "recirculation" of part of the landlords' income to peasant consumption. None of these was a direct burden on consumption in a particular time period, although in the long run, of course, they increased landlord claims to a share of national income. Only the conspicuous consumption of the wealthy, in particular their spending on imported luxuries, thereby depleting the foreign exchange resources which might otherwise have been available for the purchase of capital goods, was an "exhaustive" expenditure, a direct drain on the domestic product.

The experience of China's agriculture in the first decade of the People's Republic should be evidence enough that while substantial social change may have been a necessary condition for sustained increases in output, it was far from being a sufficient one. Even with the post-1958 increased emphasis on investment in agriculture, China's farm output still lags. The problems of supplying better seed stock, adequate fertilizer and water, optimum cropping patterns, and mechanization at critical points of labor shortage have not been easily met. In sum, the whole experience of the first three-quarters of the twentieth century suggests that only with institutional reorganization *and* large doses of advanced technological inputs could China's agrarian problem be solved.

This brings me to Dr. Elvin's "High-level Equilibrium Trap." Again, it supposes—correctly—a major qualitative distinction between traditional and modern economic growth, which Professor Lippit explicitly—and incorrectly—denies. An exclusively "technological" analysis of China's failure to industrialize before 1949 is, as I have just stated, as unsatisfactory as sole reliance on a "distributionist" explanation. We need both—and both carefully pursued. In the present context, the high-level equilibrium trap offers us one useful intermediate tool with which to understand precisely *how* the class and social structure of Qing China actually functioned at particular times and places to obstruct the passage from premodern to modern growth. Merely to state that it did so, because it was in the interest of the Confucian elite to preserve what they had, and to go no further with an elaboration of the actual historical institutions and processes by means of which this conservative goal was supported and implemented is megahistory unredeemed in its fecklessness.

Similar paragraphs might be addressed to the relationship between social structure (including the kinship system of traditional China) and underdevelopment, the effect of imperialism (see Feuerwerker, *The Foreign Establishment in China in the Early Twentieth Century),* and the role of the Ming and Qing state and bureaucracy. But I have consumed enough space for the rather simple point that I set out to make after reading Professor Lippit's "The Development of Underdevelopment in China." Let us undertake substantive studies of China's actual social and economic history which draw on all the theoretical resources that we can muster and are based on full use of the enormous contemporary sources that await sophisticated exploitation. We already know that late-Qing and republican China was "poor" and remained so while Europe, the United States, and Japan developed their economies. And we have long understood that both the bureaucratic and nonbureaucratic elite of this epoch were part of the obstacle to modern economic growth in China. Do we then know enough? Hardly. Deeper knowledge and understanding, which will enhance us both intellectually and morally, require an approach far different—and probably far more difficult—than the one I have treated so unkindly in these pages.

Albert Feuerwerker, Professor of History at the University of Michigan, has published a number of studies on China's modern economic history, most recently Economic Trends in the Republic of China, 1912-1949 *(1977).*

Development of Underdevelopment or Underdevelopment of Development in China

ANDRE GUNDER FRANK
University of East Anglia

These comments are not by a China specialist but come from someone who has been concerned with world capitalist development and the development of underdevelopment within it. In the comments that follow, therefore, the evaluation of the content of Lippit's argument about China will largely be left to the China specialists; while here we will concentrate on the construction of the argument about the development of underdevelopment. To begin with, we may question whether the title Mr. Lippit chooses for his essay is even appropriate for the argument he constructs.

Mr. Lippit does well in examining the theses that are "more obscurantist than explanatory" (as he terms one of them, though the same term applies equally to the others), and he does more than well to reject them on grounds of their lack of scientific foundation. In their universal versions (and also their applications to other case studies) the Rostowian stage theory beginning with "traditional" society, the Parsonian (pseudo-Weberian) theory of pattern variables including family structure and culture, the Leibensteinian low- and Schultzian high-level equilibrium trap theory, and the Nurskian-Myrdalian vicious circles have all long since shown to be a-, indeed anti-, historical and therein already scientifically unacceptable as vehicles for the explanation of any social process and development (and non- or underdevelopment) [Frank, 1967, 1970]. They obscure more than they explain. Moreover, their common antihistorical obscurantism is no historical accident: all of them have been politically motivated to do ideological battle on one side, the right. Rostow subtitled *Stages of Economic Growth: A Non-Communist Manifesto* (and he might more accurately have said "anti-") before he went on to be the hawkiest architect of escalation, including bombing the dikes, against Vietnam (Frank, 1967). Parsons sought "to expel Marxism from consideration as a sociology" (Gouldner, 1970: 189) and thought he had succeeded: "In sociology today, to be a Marxian . . . is not a tenable position" (Parsons 1967, 135). Through his emphasis on "human capital," Schultz sought to give ideological cover to (in Che Guevara's words) the "latrinization of Latin America" while he was Chairman of the Department of Economics at the University of Chicago, which has become world famous (or notorious) for his like-minded colleague, Milton Friedman, who is responsible for the ultrareactionary "monetarism" theory and "shock treatment" in Chile (Frank, 1974, 1976a). It is not correct and would not be fair to place Myrdal and his vicious circles in the same antiscientific and reactionary category with the other three. Myrdal's still ahistorical intent and function, instead, is more reformist, but still antirevolutionary (Frank, 1970). (One may wonder why Lippit does not also review other important unsatisfactory theories, such as Max Weber's study of world religions, including China, to confirm his thesis on "the Protestant Ethic and the Spirit of Capitalism" and Barrington Moore's study of the "Origins of Totalitarianism and Democracy" through the analysis of agrarian systems.)

The application of these theories to the case of China by these theorists' disciples (intentional and explicit or otherwise, which is not meant to deny the historical scholarship of a Fairbank) necessarily carries these theories' universal original unscientific, antihistorical, and politically conservative or reactionary sins into the study of China. And this sinological application in a Western pekinological age largely before Kissinger, Nixon and of course Zhou En-lai again opened the door, is not accidental either, though it is paradoxical. For empirically, and therefore also theoretically, the Chinese Revolution and its historical development itself have disproved these obscurantist theories and have demonstrated that traditional family structure and circular equilibrium traps have *not* been the obstacles to Chinese development since—that is, because of—the Revolution and therefore still less the causes of Chinese underdevelopment before the Revolution. But precisely because of this Revolution, cold war containment policy long took refuge in obscurantist ostrichlike denials of its existence and significance in vain attempts to combat it by keeping not only the economic and diplomatic but also the scientific door shut. It was thus that the historical materialist political economic King of Denmark was excluded from the scientific study of Hamlet in China both for the past and for the present. Lippit does well to reject this scientific and political obscurantism and to reopen the door to the scientific study of China's past along with so many eminent colleagues in China and elsewhere.

Turning to Lippit's own much more fruitful attempt at analysis, we may question whether "The Development of Underdevelopment in China" is an appropriate title for what he says and intends to do. In Lippit's initial historical sketch and in some of his later analysis, China appears to be stable, with some decline until about 1500 and some recovery thereafter, and almost stagnant without significant historical development between about 1300 and 1800 or 1400 and 1900, using per capita agricultural product as an index. This interpretation comes perilously close to the thesis of mythical "traditional" society and stability, which Lippit rightly rejects in his discussion of theory. Indeed, the century-long vagueness or uncertainty at both the beginning and end of the period already render questionable the characterization in which neither development nor underdevelopment supposedly took place. But if there was not much of either, then why the title "development of underdevelopment"—unless it is intended to refer only to the most recent imperial and republican period, on which the analysis indeed concentrates. Moreover, this reading makes development and underdevelopment appear—as in the obscurantist theories—merely comparative or relative. But as Lippit correctly points out, development and underdevelopment, and thus all the more so one *of* the other, also imply "a relationship of inequality" between China and other parts of the world. Lippit, however, makes no effort to investigate whether such a relationship existed and much less to examine any possible causes and consequences thereof for this half millennium before the nineteenth century. Indeed, Lippit hardly considers how China developed historically, and much less why it did so, before the most recent century and a half. We shall have to return to this question, and particularly to that of China's relations with the outside world, in our discussion of world development below. But in summary so far, according to Lippit and contrary to his title, there is no development of underdevelopment in China before the nineteenth century.

Is there since, and if so, how and why? According to the reading of Chinese history by Lippit (and those he criticizes!), the *internal* dynamic—or more precisely the lack of it—of Chinese development and its domestic manifestations continued through the nineteenth century and half of the twentieth substantially as it had during the five centuries before. Indeed, "most decisively, China showed no signs of a vigorous industrial development policy prior to 1949." In this major respect, then, right up to the final days of the Republic and Revolution, Lippit finds no "development of underdevelopment in China."

However, in the nineteenth and twentieth centuries, Lippit does see some unmistakable, important dependent development of underdevelopment of China through its external relations with the Western imperialist powers and Japan and their domestic effects, some far-reaching others supposedly not so much, within China itself. No objective observer, scientific or lay, can deny these causes and consequences from the opium trade, through the treaty ports to the Open Door. Western historians from Tawney to Lattimore have stressed them, and fellow invited commentators, John King Fairbank and Albert Feuerwerker, have devoted much of their lives to studying them; so there is no need to recount them here. But, Lippit argues, "to recognize the importance of this relationship and to assign it primary causal responsibility are two different things." "Primary causal responsibility" for what? "The impact of the West cannot be assigned primary responsibility for the *development of underdevelopment in China*" (my emphasis); or "Western support for reactionary government . . . was not decisive in *inhibiting* economic *development*"? Which is it, inhibiting development from non- or undevelopment or producing underdevelopment? There is a decisive difference between the two for the "dependence theory" of "development of underdevelopment" according to which, as Lippit himself rightly stresses, development and underdevelopment are not just relatively more or less, but are in a relationship to each other within a single wider system. Therefore, Lippit's easy passage from one to the other is an inadmissible slight of hand within this "theory" on which he draws in part for support and in part to discard it again as unsatisfactory (which it may well be, but not for the reason Lippit claims).

Lippit argues that there was some external development of underdevelopment in China, but that it was not decisive because for internal reasons China would not have developed anyway (so that really there was no decisive development of underdevelopment in China after all—so why the title?). But those of us who have stressed the decisive importance of external dependence and its internal structure and consequences for the development of underdevelopment and thereby preventing the development of development, have never claimed that the absence of such dependence is an ipso facto guarantee of development or even of a will or capacity therefor. Other un- (*not* under-) developed societies were not dependent and nonetheless did not experience capitalist development due to other—internal—factors during certain periods. In Asia, Thailand and Japan fall in this category, and elsewhere some parts of Africa and Latin America. In the course of world history some of these regions and societies subsequently did become dependent and developed underdevelopment. Thailand after World War II is a notorious case; other regions suffered a similar fate earlier, among them China. None of the cases of dependent capitalist development of underdevelopment could have—as the theoretical argument went—or have—as the historical record shows—subsequently experienced capitalist development in the Western sense. Japan did develop, once internal conditions changed appropriately from the Tokugawa period through the Meiji Restoration, not because of Levy's supposed difference of family structure or other Parsonian pattern variables, not even because of differences in commercialization between Tokugawa Japan and Qing China (except insofar as this difference helped determine the course of internal change itself). Instead, as Norman (1940) has magisterially shown, Japan was not—and did not subsequently become—dependent, and therefore *was* able to launch such capitalist development; while in China dependent development of underdevelopment decisively prevented such capitalist development, no matter what internal conditions might or might not have become, for instance through the Taiping Revolution, the Boxer Rebellion, or the Sun Yat-sen Republic. Their initial programs say little about what they might or might not have developed into, so that Western help in crushing the former was decisive, when at the time of the first capitalist development it might still have been possible in the absence of dependence, while the success of the last was no longer relevant in the face of the by then insuperable obstacle of dependence, insuperable that is except through anticapitalist socialist revolution and noncapitalist development.

External dependence, and all it implies, therefore did not cause the internal conditions in China that inhibited development or caused the underdevelopment of development in China for centuries. The class structure and the bureaucratic economy that Lippit, in part following Balazs, analyzes were no doubt substantially responsible, though much of what Lippit says and we know about China in this regard is rather reminiscent of mercantilist Europe and even of the neoimperialist United States and the contemporary world; so that the decisive differences still remain unclear. But to the extent to which these internal differences were not decisive for inhibiting development or might have ceased to be so, external dependence and its internal implications in China became decisive in the nineteenth and twentieth centuries in generating the development of underdevelopment in China, irrespective of internal attempts at change, some of which it prevented. Thus, China was confronted with the real alternative of continued capitalist underdevelopment at the hands of world imperialism allied with the Chinese "comprador" bourgeoisie and increasing misery for its people following the Indian example, or socialist revolution and development, setting an example for the world (which is belatedly now admired even by some erstwhile obscurantist ostriches).

Lippit's comparative class and political economic analysis and the alternatives he poses to the development of underdevelopment are a decisive step forward compared to his justly criticized predecessors's erring in the woods. But all of this analysis, including that of the development of underdevelopment by the present author on which Lippit draws, are still unsatisfactorily handicapped in at least two important ways.

(1) They (have to) suppose a hypothetical never never land in which development and underdevelopment would be or might have been different—"independent" development?—if the world were square instead of round, in which we try to explain what happened to China in terms of what might have happened if things had been different there and/or compared with elsewhere. This procedure departs from reality "Wie es eigentlich gewesen ist" in the nonderogatory realistic sense of that phrase. Among those Lippit cites, Fairbank has made a magisterial contribution to clarifying "how it really was," even though "to its author [it] is a mere antechamber to a whole unwritten library, bursting with problems awaiting exploration" (Fairbank, 1969: xii), and although his political commitment seems to have excluded posing himself the real theoretical implications for Lippit's analytical problem of Fairbank's own historical research. We can only ask for more of both.

(2) Second, this approach is partially unsatisfactory precisely because it is partial, and analyzes only China and the effects on it *from* the outside and/or in comparison with other parts of the

world. What we need—though the Chinese themselves may be the last to admit it—is historical analysis of the *whole* world, of its *single* historical process, and of the place of China and other parts of the world *in* it—and that over a much longer time span than the part of the nineteenth and twentieth centuries effectively analyzed by Lippit (Wallerstein, 1974). How did the world develop, and why did it develop as it did—with China in it? To pose the question this way is not an attempt to elude the question of Chinese development itself, but to pose it differently, more usefully, in terms of "historical research progresses backward, not forward," as Fairbank (1969: ix) pleads (Frank, 1978a: preface). From a Chinese point of view "during the last thousand years, in short the Chinese people have been almost half the time under alien domination. Barbarian rule has been an integral part of their life" (Fairbank, 1969: 8). On the other hand, Lippit introduces his study with a brief account of the then unrivalled advances of Chinese development—and contributions to humanity—until the fourteenth century and cites the Chinese emperor's much later oft-quoted letter to King George III saying we have everything we need. In the meantime, Chinese had crossed the Indian Ocean with vast fleets (exceeding European ones in size four centuries later) and traded into Africa earlier and more effectively than the Europeans or even the Ottomans and Arabs. Then they withdrew and left the field open to others, except in Southeast Asia where they were subsequently also replaced, in part voluntarily, in part by economic and military force. Why—in terms of internal Chinese imperial-landlord-merchant interests and relations of power—and how did this happen? (To engage in a bit more "if the world were square" speculation, what would have happened if the Chinese, like Longfellow's Arabs, had not folded their tents and silently slipped away; what if they had colonialized us?) Then, while particular parts of the West developed and expanded at different times and into specific places, including some in the East, Japan closed itself off from abroad almost entirely after 1636, while China permitted only limited contact under specified conditions. Since then and until our days, China has not been at the center of world economic, political, and cultural development and has occupied a singular intermediary role between the Western powers on the one side and their Asian colonies and junior partners on the other, beginning with the Spanish Manila Galleon, Portuguese and Dutch Far Eastern intra-Asian trade in the sixteenth and seventeenth centuries, and then escalating in the late eighteenth and early nineteenth centuries to the British opium trade between India and China, which was initially designed to help defray their balance of trade deficit with both (Frank, 1978a). Even in the classical imperialist period of the nineteenth and twentieth centuries China's semicolonial economic position in the world was peculiar and almost unique among those then suffering the development of underdevelopment, in that unlike other such "Third World" countries (which had a consistent merchandise export surplus) China had a merchandise import surplus with the developed countries of Europe derived from her entreport trade position between the colonial powers and their colonies elsewhere in Asia (Frank, 1976b). The suggestion is not that these "external" relations of China should weigh more heavily in our study of China's or the world's history than China's changing "internal" conditions, but that any adequate analysis of Chinese and world history, let alone any theory of development, must analyze these historical changes in relation to each other within the compass of the single and temporally simultaneous but multiform historical process of which they were and are all related parts. Like Marx, we must stand Hegel on his head, and not only with regard to the development of China.

REFERENCES

FAIRBANK, JOHN KING (1969) Trade and Diplomacy on the China Coast. The Opening of the Treaty Ports, 1842-1854. Stanford: Stanford Univ. Press.
FRANK, ANDRE GUNDER (1978a) World Accumulation, 1492-1789. New York: Monthly Review.

——— (1978b) Dependent Accumulation and Underdevelopment. London: Macmillan.

——— (1976a) Economic Genocide in Chile. Monetarist Theory Versus Humanity. Nottingham: Spokesman Books.

——— (1976b) "Multilateral mechandise trade imbalances and uneven economic development." J. of European Economic History 5, 2 (Fall) Rome.

——— (1974) "On the roots of development and underdevelment in the New World: Smith and Marx vs. the Weberians." International Rev. of Sociology, II Series 10, 2-3 (August-December) Rome.

——— (1970) "The wealth and poverty of nations. Even heretics remain bound by traditional thought." Economic and Pol. Weekly (July) special number. Bombay. Also in A. G. Frank (forthcoming) Critica y Anti-Critica. Madrid: Ediciones Zero.

——— (1967) "The sociology of development and the underdevelopment of sociology." Catalyst 3 (Summer). Also in A. G. Frank, Latin America: Underdevelopment or Revolution. New York: Monthly Review.

GOULDNER, ALVIN W. (1970) The Coming Crisis of Western Sociology. New York: Basic Books.

LATTIMORE, OWEN (1960) "The industrial impact on China, 1800-1950." First International Conference on Economic History, Stockholm. The Hague: Mouton.

MOORE, BARRINGTON Jr. (1966) Social Origins of Dictatorship and Democracy, Lord and Peasant in the Making of the Modern World. Boston: Beacon.

MYRDAL, GUNNAR (1957) Economic Theory and Underdeveloped Regions. London: Duckworth.

NORMAN, E. HERBERT (1940) Japan's Emergence as a Modern State. New York: Institute of Pacific Relations. Also in John W. Dower (ed.) Origins of the Modern Japanese State. Selected Writings of E. H. Norman. New York: Pantheon.

PARSONS, TALCOTT (1967) Sociological Theory and Modern Society. New York: Free Press.

——— (1951) The Social System. Glencoe: Free Press.

ROSTOW, WALT WHITMAN (1962) The Stages of Economic Growth. A Non-Communist Manifesto. Cambridge: Cambridge University Press.

TAWNEY, R. H. (1966) Land and Labour in China. Boston: Beacon Press.

WALLERSTEIN, IMMANUEL (1974) The Modern World System. New York: Academic Press.

WEBER, MAX (1958) The Protestant Ethic and the Spirit of Capitalism. New York: Scribners.

——— (1951) The Religion of China. Glencoe: Free Press.

Andre Gunder Frank received his Ph.D. in economics from the University of Chicago in 1957. In August 1978 he takes up the post of Professor of Development Studies, University of East Anglia. In recent years, Dr. Frank has been studying the economic, social, and political history of capitalism as a single world-embracing system. Among his recent publications are Accumulation, Dependence and Underdevelopment *(1977) and* World Accumulation, 1492-1789 *(1977).*

The Roots of Underdevelopment

Reflections on the Chinese Experience

KEITH GRIFFIN

Queen Elizabeth House, and
Institute of Commonwealth Studies

The history of the world, for the last five centuries, in so far as it has significance, has been European history.
—Hugh Trevor-Roper

It has often been claimed, from Hegel to Trevor-Roper, that the underdeveloped countries have no history or if they do, that it is of no significance. Sensible people now know these claims to be false. Indeed it could be said that a large part of the history of mankind, from the ancient invention of writing to the contemporary invention of new forms of social organization, has been written in China, the world's largest underdeveloped country.

China, of course, has not always been underdeveloped. In fact, during a period when Europe was mired in the squalor of the Middle Ages, "China was incontestably the most advanced country of the time" (Gernet, 1970: 18). It is the great merit of Lippit's essay that it places China's underdevelopment in historical context and increases our understanding of the process by which China ceased to be the most advanced nation and became one of the most backward. Strange to say, the issue raised by Lippit has been relatively negelected for it has been only in recent years, thanks in large part to the pioneering work of Paul Baran and A. G. Frank, that scholars have begun to abandon the earlier view of underdevelopment as the original state of nature and to see it instead as a product of social and economic forces.

Exactly how underdevelopment is produced remains an area of considerable controversy. Given our present ignorance, careful studies of the historical experience of particular countries are of more than usual value: not only do we learn from them of the country concerned but, through the accumulation of such studies, it may be possible gradually to induce the general processes at work. No single theory of underdevelopment can yet command assent. For the time being all we can hope to agree upon are the ingredients which contribute to a process of underdevelopment; the proportions in which the ingredients are mixed no doubt will vary from one society to another. In particular, the relative importance of internal and external elements will differ from one situation to another and, in truth, from one observer to another.

There can be no doubt, however, that on occasion the external ingredients have been decisive. Thus, for example, societies and their economies have been partially destroyed and underdeveloped through the importation of exotic diseases (as in the South Pacific), through foreign conquest (as in western South America) or as a consequence of incorporation into an unfavorable trading arrangement (as with the slave trade in West Africa). These illustrations are not mere theoretical possibilities. They happened; the results are well-known and can still be seen today. The question is whether phenomena such as these are systemic or episodic, i.e., whether they are freakish, random events impossible to foresee or the predictable outcome of a particular international system.

The truth is we do not know. But we do know that China was subjected to the same sorts of external pressures that beset other nations and contributed to their underdevelopment. Thus China was incorporated into a nefarious trading arrangement against her will and in exchange for a harmful substance (opium) was obliged to give up useful products, submit herself to the injurious effects of drug disease and dissipate part of her economic surplus by transferring silver abroad. Similarly, in a typical example of

Orwellian double-talk, China was forced to pay indemnities to foreigners for disservices rendered. Again, China was afflicted by foreign interference in her government, by military intervention by the West, and finally by partial conquest by Japan.

No one denies that these things occurred, and Lippit, moreover, adds to the list. Few deny that there was a certain amount of deindustrialization in China, although it probably was not as significant as in India (Bagchi, 1976). No one denies that the mass of the population remained extremely poor for a very long time, or that living standards fell sharply in the three decades before the revolution.[1] The facts, broadly, are not in dispute; what is in dispute is the connection, if any, between the facts.

There are six possible positions one can adopt as to the relationship between processes creating and perpetuating underdevelopment in China and foreign involvement in the economy and polity of China. First, it could be argued that there is no connection between the two, just as there is no connection between, say, the British presence in the Falkland Islands and the poor performance of Argentina's economy. The denial of any relationship of cause and effect in the case of China, however, amounts almost to nihilism. In some respects it is similar to the view that history consists essentially of a series of accidents, just "one damn thing after another," and is equally unsatisfactory. Second, there is the classical liberal position that on balance foreign intercourse is beneficial to all participating parties, raising levels of income and promoting development everywhere. Just as trade between England and Portugal was of mutual advantage, so too presumably, relations between China and the West (and Japan) contributed positively to Chinese development. If nonetheless underdevelopment increased, this must be because domestic forces were so strong that they neutralized the beneficent impulses originating abroad. This liberal position, however, despite its impressive pedigree, is hardly persuasive, if for no other reason than the fact that throughout most of the nineteenth century involuntary purchases of opium constituted the largest import into China.

At the other extreme, third, is the crude imperialist thesis that all the ills of China can be attributed to the foreign devils. Lippit effortlessly demolishes this position. A more subtle position, fourth, and one which may be close to Lippit's own, is that the nature and content of China's relations with the rest of the world were essentially a consequence of underdevelopment rather than its cause. This seems to be the best interpretation of Lippit's closing sentence that "the development of underdevelopment in China . . . should be understood in terms of the emergence of a constellation of domestic forces inhibiting progress, into which constellation a rapacious West intruded."

A fifth view is that both the nature of China's foreign relations and the persistence of underdevelopment are a product of some third cause. Just as the application of heat to paper produces both potash and calories, so some unspecified force caused both underdevelopment in China and external vulnerability. In abstract terms this argument certainly is plausible, but as an explanation of historical events it suffers from the fact that the common cause has yet to be identified. Lastly, and perhaps more promising than the previous explanation, is the view that internal and external forces, in a process of mutual causation, interact on each other to produce underdevelopment. This is the view that I happen to hold. If this view is correct, then there is no reason in principle why it should be impossible to detect primary causal responsibility for the process of underdevelopment or to attribute relative importance to internal and external elements. In practice, of course, there are many reasons why this still is extremely difficult. The rules governing the behavior of social systems are not exactly analogous to the laws regulating chemical reactions, nor as simple, yet there is hope that one day it will be possible to assign weights to variables in interacting social processes.

Lippit's analysis focuses on the linkages between the economic surplus, technical change, and class relations. These seem to me to be the key domestic variables in the equation and his argument is persuasive. He demonstrates that the economic surplus in China was substantial, that this surplus was highly concentrated in the hands of a small ruling class, and that consequently China possessed the technical capacity for high rates of saving and capital accumulation. Investment and technical change proceeded slowly however, not because the possibilities of existing technical knowledge had been exhausted, but because China, unlike Japan, neither borrowed and adapted technology from abroad nor devoted resources to producing new technical knowledge of her own.

The reason for this, in turn, is related to the domination of Chinese society by the gentry class and their control over most of the machinery of government and the policies of the state. As in other underdeveloped countries, the major sources of high incomes were large landholdings, big business, and the senior positions in the public administration, all of which were in the possession of the gentry. Rent from land rose inexorably as growing population densities in rural areas increased the value of cultivable terrain. Higher profits in big business could be obtained more easily not by lowering costs but by obtaining greater market privileges, exploiting monopolistic power, and raising prices. Finally, office holders were able to multiply their official salaries through corruption on a vast scale.

Lippit surely is right to emphasize that in such a setting the ruling class and the state they controlled had neither the need nor the incentive to increase the nation's stock of capital or the pace of technical change. Other classes certainly had the need but lacked the means. Thus forces internal to China probably do account in large part for the process of underdevelopment. Lippit takes a slightly stronger position, however, in asserting that "the principal features of underdevelopment appeared and were sustained independently, for the most part, of the Western impact."

He may well be correct and my hesitations may well be foolish. The argument is slightly puzzling, however. For example, if internal forces account for China's descent from the world's most advanced to one of the most backward countries, something must have happened which changed the dynamics of China's development. It seems rather implausible to imply that the change in relative position is due entirely to changes in internal forces in the now developed countries and, furthermore, that these changes abroad had no significant effect on China. This argument, indeed, if pushed to an extreme, would come rather close to some of the views Lippit rebuts. Yet if forces internal to China did cause her to enter into a process of underdevelopment, when did this process begin and what were the internal changes that initiated it? It seems to me that what changed first was the world, not China, and the impact of these changes on China was adverse, provoking internal changes which interacted with external ones so as to create a cumulative process of underdevelopment.

This does not imply, of course, that in all places and at all times external forces were responsible for initiation of a downward spiral. The significance of foreign contacts for initiating and perpetuating underdevelopment is that it is not a "yes or no" issue. What is important is the nature of the contacts and the balance between elements which stimulate and those which retard development. Moreover, what is retarding in one context may be stimulating in another. For instance, private foreign investment and public foreign aid may be beneficial in one setting and harmful in another. Clearly, internal social alignments are of great importance in determining whether an external force is positive or negative. To use yet another analogy, foreign contacts are a bit like a cold shower. In some circumstances a cold shower can be invigorating whereas in others it can cause pneumonia. The temperature of the water obviously is important in determining the outcome, but so too is the general state of health of the bather. In the case of China, the temperature was low and the bather unwell.

Even if agreement cannot be reached on whether it was external or internal forces which bear primary responsibility for setting in motion a process of underdevelopment, it seems clear that the solution lies in the domestic sphere. That is, it is unlikely that underdevelopment can be arrested through attempts to change the world; it must be done by changing the politics and the economy of the country concerned. This China did, with results known to all.

IMPERALISM AND UNDERDEVELOPMENT IN CHINA

Assessing the responsibility of Western intervention for China's plight in the nineteenth and early twentieth centuries requires first understanding the nature of that plight. Confusion about this issue constitutes the chief conceptual problem—spotted by both Feuerwerker and Frank—with Lippit's essay. Both discussants challenge the essay's title on the ground that it is contradicted by the paper's implicit message that "really there was no decisive development of underdevelopment in China after all" (Frank). Frank observes that, as used by its progenitors, the very concept of "development of underdevelopment" (DUD) includes as part of its central character "the decisive importance of external dependence and its internal structure and consequences." The latter involve such phenomena as the suppression of the potential for a domestic manufacturing sector with its backward and forward linkages and its impact on the acquisition of technological knowledge and skills; specialization in primary products generally lacking such linkages; the growth of a powerful compradore class of capitalists and government officials with interests tied to those of foreign monopolies and thus antithetical to indigenous capitalist development; and so on.[1] DUD is *defined* as a process involving such phenomena of external dependence, and is quite distinct from the concept of lack of development. As Frank points out, in terms of his concept of "dependence," some societies which did not develop were spared victimization by imperialism and thus did not acquire the special characteristics of DUD. The theory of DUD specifically denies the possibility of successful and self-sustained capitalist growth because of the adverse consequences of foreign penetration. Lippit, on the other hand, argues that capitalist growth in China was thwarted by the opposition of the dominant gentry class which benefited from maintenance of the agrarian, precapitalist status quo. Logically, there is no room in Lippit's argument for DUD as a decisive element in Chinese history.

Fundamentally, Lippit's argument is that foreign penetration of China was made possible by China's internal weakness, which was in turn due chiefly to domestic class structure and its ramifications. Griffin puts Lippit's view epigrammatically: "the nature and content of China's relations with the rest of the world were essentially a consequence of underdevelopment rather than its cause." However, the same argument can be applied to *all* societies that have suffered the adverse effects of substantial foreign economic penetration, for it is a truism that had they been internally strong enough to resist successfully, they would have escaped "underdevelopment." And when they *were* strong enough (Japan) relative to the threat facing them, escape it they did.

The problem, as Frank accurately identifies it, is that the essay vacillates between addressing the question of the "development of underdevelopment" in China and the quite different question of why China did not undergo vigorous capitalist transformation and growth at least through the nineteenth century. This confusion is apparent in the fact that Lippit does not actually define "underdevelopment" in its Frankian sense until some three-quarters of the way to the end, and until that point uses the term as synonymous with lack of development relative to the advanced Western countries.

The one question originally posed by Lippit (why the development of underdevelopment in China) now divides into two. First, did foreign penetration in the nineteenth and early twentieth centuries *fundamentally* alter the nature of Chinese economy and society in the direction of "underdevelopment," e.g., by linking the majority of the peasantry closely to the international market, restructuring production to foster specialization in a few primary products for export, suppressing domestic handicrafts and manufacturing so as to create a national market for foreign manufactures; and thoroughly coopting ruling elites into the foreign economic and cultural sphere? Second: did such penetration, even if insufficient to have the above results, nevertheless play a significant role in blocking indigenous capitalist development?

Regarding the first question, we can rule out the possibility that imperialism destroyed or adversely changed the character of an already existing process of vigorous capitalist development, since it is generally agreed that China's modern economic growth "began only in response to the exogenous shock of imported foreign goods and foreign manufacturing in China" (Feuerwerker, 1976: 98). Western penetration thus provided the "cold shower" (in Griffin's phrase), but it remains to be determined whether this produced the pneumonia of Frankian "underdevelopment." As Lippit's argument implies, the answer seems to be negative, not because dependent characteristics of the class and economic structures were absent, but because they were a relatively small element in both. Thus, for example, Chinese exports did consist predominantly of tea and silk throughout the second half of the nineteeth century, a kind of specialization that "did not stimulate the production of other goods in China" (Dernberger, 1975: 34), and that brought great hardship to many peasants when Japanese competition began to preempt the demand for these industries. But exports were very small relative to gross domestic product, so that even though their composition was not conducive to stimulating growth, from the viewpoint of the economy as a whole they represented only a very minor concession to specialization for the world market.

The structure of China's imports was certainly influenced by the superior economic and military power of the trading "partners." Opium, the largest single import until the 1890s (Feuerwerker, 1968: 70), would not have been imported legally at all had the Chinese government retained full sovereignty. Other principal imports, such as cotton goods, cereals, sugar and kerosene, catered to final demand and had negligible stimulative impact on production within China (Dernberger, 1975: 34-35). Some of these goods (kerosene, cotton yarn) replaced domestic handicraft products, with serious consequences for the workers involved. However, the very importance of opium in nineteenth century imports is a symbol of the inability of the Western countries to break into the China market on any substantial scale (Esherick, 1972: 10). Imports, like exports, were small in proportion to GDP, and their adverse impact on domestic handicrafts could not have been too great, since the latter as a whole appear not to have declined from the late nineteenth century until the 1930s, when they still accounted for 7½% of NDP (Liu and Yeh, 1965: 66). Moreover, as Lippit (citing Perkins) points out, many domestic handicrafts were not subject to competition at all,[2] while others competed effectively in most areas of the country. Finally, it would be a gross distortion to treat the ruling elites of late nineteenth and early twentieth century China—even the compradores—as identifying mainly with the aspirations and interests of the foreigners (Hao, 1970; Bergère, 1968).

Therefore, the limited relative size and penetration of the foreign presence makes it difficult to characterize Chinese economy and society as a whole in terms of Frankian "underdevelopment": "China was relatively successful in resisting the impulse of the Western bourgeoisie to 'nestle everywhere, settle everywhere, establish connections everywhere.' She was never reduced to the status of an Egypt, an India or an Argentina" (Esherick, 1972: 10; see also Murphey, 1970). This, it seems to me, is the real significance of much of Lippit's argument with respect to the limited impact of the Western presence.

Even if one reaches the provisional judgment that penetration was insufficient to warrant regarding early twentieth century China as "underdeveloped," this does not by itself absolve the Western powers and Japan of responsibility for impeding modern economic growth in China. Here, it would seem, the evidence of limited foreign penetration relative to the economy as a whole is beside the point. It is precisely because of Lippit's convincing case that China's relative backwardness as of the mid-nineteenth century was a product of internal circumstances, and that the forces of indigenous modern economic growth were weak, that a very limited such penetration *could* have been enough to block the possibility of development (although we are now on perilous counterfactual ground). Lippit, with the weight of the preponderance of the field behind him here, vigorously rejects this possibility, but it is worth raising a couple of questions about his argument.

First, while acknowledging that foreigners dominated the modern sector, and especially heavy industry, Lippit repeats C. M. Hou's argument that Chinese firms could not have been seriously disadvantaged by this, since they were "at least able to hold their own" in terms of their share of manufacturing as a whole. Feuerwerker (1976: 92) seems to have come around to this view as well, but I admit to finding more convincing his earlier criticism of it as being "quite misleading":

> From the available evidence, it might just as reasonably be argued that in the absence of foreign competition Chinese firms might have grown even faster and carried the whole modern sector of the economy along with them [Feuerwerker, 1968: 17].

In other words, the stability of foreign and Chinese market shares *by itself* has no analytical significance for the question at issue.

Second, Lippit employs an argument also used by Dernberger (1975: 44), namely, that there "was nothing to prevent" the Chinese government from subsidizing native industries as a substitute for the tariff protection denied them by the foreign powers. This strikes me as a naive argument in its assumption that the powers would cheerfully have permitted the subversion of their successful policy of denying protection to Chinese industry. As Moulder (1977: 194-195) shows, the Chinese government did in fact make such attempts, but they "were not as successful as they were in Japan, primarily because the Western powers refused to cooperate." It may well be that the Chinese government could have been more forceful in devising counter-penetration strategems, but the issue cannot be settled on the basis of the inherently implausible assumption that there was "nothing to prevent" such policies.

This brings us to the important issue of the impact of foreign intervention on the state. Lippit writes: "Finally, and most decisively, China showed no signs of a vigorous industrial development policy prior to 1949." Few would disagree that the late Qing government was basically incapable of fostering the economic, legal, and educational institutions required for the sustenance of modern enterprise (Feuerwerker, 1969: 43). The question is whether the foreign presence, in both supporting and simultaneously weakening, constraining, and delegitimizing the government, significantly hindered progressive change in these respects. Moulder (1977) argues that it did and Lippit that it did not, but both (in my view) unconvincingly: the former because Moulder does not provide much evidence that the Chinese government might have been capable of fashioning successful development even if it had not been "incorporated" and "dismantled" to the extent it was; and the latter because Lippit seems altogether unconcerned with the counterfactual problem. He seems certain that, whatever political course China might have taken in the absence of the complex Western and Japanese intervention, it would *not* have included rapid evolution toward a vigorous development policy. But at least with respect to the period after the Opium Wars, it is circular reasoning to hold that foreign penetration did not block development because there were "no signs of a vigorous industrial development policy" to block. One could as well move in the opposite direction and ascribe the absence of such signs to penetration. Establishing which view is correct requires a thorough analysis of the impact of penetration on the Chinese state. Lippit provides chiefly the correct but insufficient observation that foreign support was not decisive in perpetuating the dynasty.

It should be apparent from the above that I regard the question of imperialism's relative responsibility for the lack of modern economic growth in China to be a more complex and intractable one than Lippit's treatment or Feuerwerker's comments imply. My own "position" (in the sense of framework for thinking about the problem) is closest to Griffin's sixth (and his own) view, namely, "that internal and external forces, in a process of mutual causation, interact" to block development. It may be possible in principle, as Griffin suggests, to attribute relative importance to these two elements. I share Griffin's feeling that, on balance, internal forces were of primary importance; also, his skepticism about Lippit's stronger position discounting the Western impact almost to insignificance; and finally, his telling observation regarding the importance of internal social alignments in determining the positive or negative effect of an external force. This point is ignored by Frank when he states that "in China dependent development of underdevelopment decisively prevented such capitalist development, *no matter what internal conditions might or might not have developed* " (emphasis added), a position that also cries out for supportive evidence other than the inconsequential Western contribution to the defeat of the Taiping Revolution. Indeed, the most significant conclusion from all this is that the relations between the state, the class structure, and the foreign impact on China seem still to offer a fertile and potentially productive area for concrete historical investigation.

SURPLUS

Virtually all societies produce an economic surplus above the subsistence requirements of their populations, as Feuerwerker observes. Study of a society's mode or modes of production, extraction, and utilization of this surplus is certainly necessary for understanding social and economic change. Mark Elvin, who has previously dealt with this issue in a very enlightening way, here takes the position that " 'surplus theories' of economic history such as Profession Lippit's" are based on the "very questionable premise [that] the leisure-preference of the labor-force is zero." What Elvin appears to mean is that a society's total output—and therefore the potential surplus above some given level of necessary consumption—will depend upon socioeconomic conditions, and cannot validly be assumed constant when such conditions change. This is certainly a correct observation. Elvin is further correct in pointing out the possibility that output (and therefore potential surplus) *may* fall under some kinds of socioeconomic change, e.g., with the elimination of rent.

But Elvin goes beyond these unobjectionable points to argue that output *is likely* to fall when exploitation is reduced, and that the opposite assertion implies "zero leisure-preference" on the part of the labor force. This argument is mistaken, even within the narrow and artificial limits of the assumptions used to state it, and most especially if more realistic assumptions are introduced.

Elvin, following Chayanov, sees the peasant as determining his labor input (and therefore his production) by the equilibrium condition that "the output to be gained from further exertions was not judged to be a reasonable exchange for the irksomeness of the extra effort required." The following equation expresses this equilibrium condition:

$$MPL = \frac{MDL}{MUY}$$

where MPL (marginal product of labor) is the addition to output produced by the last unit of labor performed, MDL (marginal disutility of labor) is the "extra irksomeness" of the last unit of labor performed, and MUY (marginal utility of income) is the desirability to the peasant of the last unit of income received. The right-hand side (the "real cost of labor") tells us how many units of income must be offered to just induce the peasant to perform the last unit of labor.[3] In equilibrium, the income produced by the last such unit (i.e., MPL) must just equal this amount.[4]

Let us now assume the peasant is in equilibrium *under exploitation conditions*, i.e., producing output O_e and paying a rent of S_1 in Elvin's diagram. Elvin states that, in contradistinction to the alleged assumptions of "surplus theory historians," if exploitation were to disappear (eliminating the rent), output would fall. Now, the disappearance of rent would raise peasant income, and, if marginal utility of income is falling as income rises, then ceteris paribus the "real cost of labor" would increase and exceed the marginal product of labor, thus calling forth a reduction in work and output as Elvin predicts. On the other hand, if marginal utility of income is constant over the relevant range of incomes, no change in the real cost of labor would occur and no change in work and output.

The ceteris paribus assumption implicit in Elvin's analysis is arbitrary. If it is relaxed, any number of things can happen. For instance, the increase in income occasioned by the elimination of rent may improve the peasant's nutritional level and health and thus reduce the "irksomeness" of any given amount of labor (i.e., lower the MDL schedule). This of course would tend to reduce the "real cost of labor" (MDL/MUY), and if it did so sufficiently to compensate or overcompensate for any increase in MUY, work and output would remain constant or increase. Note that we already have two conditions under which output would *not* fall with the elimination of exploitation: MUY constant, and "irksomeness" reduced. Neither one involves "zero leisure-preference" on the part of the work force.

However, the range of variables that must be considered is much wider still. Elvin does not specify the conditions under which exploitation disappears, yet these and the new arrangements replacing tenancy will be of paramount importance in determining the impact on output. Land reforms on historical record have occurred under a great variety of conditions and with widely varying effects on production. Consider briefly three cases in which output rose.

China's land reform of the early 1950s gave rise to a sizable increase in peasant consumption, yet at the same time contributed substantially to increasing the national investment rate (Lippit, 1974: 138 and passim). Its short-run impact on farm output was not entirely positive, however. General disruption, inadequate supplies of rural credit, and problems of livestock maintenance did not help production. Yet Perkins (1975: 108) ventures the opinion that such negative influences "were probably outweighed or at least matched by the elimination of rented land held under conditions of insecure tenure and other undesirable contractual arrangements." In any event, output rose continuously during and immediately after the reform (Lippit, 1974: 141-142; Chao, 1970: 304-305). In the longer run, by its contribution to industrial-ization and its political impact on the countryside, the land reform can be interpreted as helping to establish the precon-ditions for collectivization and for the subsequent policy of tech-nical transformation that came in during the 1960s.

In Taiwan, land reform was followed by a set of government policies concerning taxes, fees, land payments, terms of trade between agriculture and industry, and investment, which kept peasants under pressure to increase output while providing them with better incentives to do so and with improved access to physical and financial resources (Griffin, 1974: 122-126). Output thus went up. Furthermore, the use of produced surplus was altered; unlike the case before the land reform, surplus extracted from the agricultural sector was now returned to it in the form of state investment, subsidies, and so on, causing agricultural output to rise for any given amount of labor input and making possible higher surpluses subsequently.

The land reform measures undertaken in early Meiji Japan probably substantially reduced the average tax burden on landowners (Nakamura, 1966: 160-163). Nevertheless, output rose thereafter (although the rate of increase remains in dispute). Abolition of feudal restrictions made possible a reallocation of resources along more efficient lines and wider diffusion of superior seeds and techniques. Moreover, the Meiji tax unlike the Tokugawa was fixed according to land value and thus predictable, which improved incentives by ensuring that a proportion of additional output would be retained by the landowner (Ohkawa and Rosovsky, 1973: 13-14). Meiji reforms resulted in a substantial redistribution of surplus from the former ruling class to the landowner, whose propensity to save was higher (Nakamura, 1966: 156-169). This resulted in some greater investment in agriculture and much more in industry. In the long run, industrial growth permitted not only the absorption of labor from the countryside, but also the development of such modern inputs as chemical fertilizer, an increasingly important source of growth in farm productivity.

It is clear from these examples that rent or tax reductions *can* give rise to increases in output under widely divergent modes and relations of production. Crucial in determining the impact of institutional changes on output is what happens simultaneously to such factors as the distribution of land, tools, animals, and equipment among the farm population; the peasant's risk position, access to material and financial resources and incentive to produce and invest, as determined by the above changes and by government tax policies and movements of relative prices; the degree of relief from previous labor obligations to the landlord; and so on.

All such factors lie ouside the framework of Elvin's analysis, yet without considering them it is impossible to predict the behavior of output. The point of estimating the surplus under one set of socioeconomic conditions (apart from its intrinsic historical interest) is not to advance a spurious claim for its immutability, but to establish a benchmark that, in conjunction with study of the above sorts of factors, may provide some insight into the alternative possibilities under changed conditions.

Feuerwerker takes a different tack, pointing out that since the identification of income as surplus depends upon its use, property incomes that are recycled to the peasantry by means of land purchases (net of sales) or loans (net of repayments), or that are removed from circulation by hoarding (net of dishoarding), cannot be considered part of the surplus. This is quite true, as is the opposite proposition (not mentioned by Feuerwerker) that net property sales by landlords, repayment of loans, and dis-hoarding would enlarge the surplus in a given year (Riskin, 1975: 59, 68-69). But Feuerwerker confuses the issue by referring to it as one of "uses of the surplus" rather than of definition of it. For example, net peasant repayments over new loans extended would enlarge the surplus even though some new loans were being made. Feuerwerker is right to say that we know little about this question for 1933 (or other years), and this serves to warn against creating the spurious impression of precision in estimating surplus.[5] But rather than repudiating the concept of surplus, such problems should only stimulate the research needed to make future estimates better.

THE HIGH-LEVEL EQUILIBRIUM TRAP

This concept, pioneered by Mark Elvin and by Radha Sinha, has indeed had an influential career, as Lippit indicates. In one respect, it closely resembles Schultz's (1964) thesis, and it is in this respect that Dernberger (1975) and Perkins (1975) have used it and that Lippit criticizes it. However, Elvin (1973) is far more ambitious in what he seeks to explain with it than was Schultz, who argued that peasants typically do not invest much because they have reached an equilibrium position in which further investment in the traditional technology is discouraged by the low expected rate of return. The problem in Schultz's case is how to make new, modern, science-based farm technology available to the peasantry at reasonable prices. Elvin, on the other hand, seeks to explain by means of the high-level equilibrium trap the absence of dynamic technological change on an economy-wide scale. Since economists have not paid much attention to this more interesting aspect of the argument, it is worthwhile to quote it at some length:

> [I]n late traditional China economic forces developed in such a way as to make profitable invention more and more difficult. With falling surplus in agriculture, and so *falling per capita income and per capita demand*, with *cheapening labour but increasingly expensive resources and capital*, with farming and transport technologies so good that no simple improvements could be made, rational strategy for peasant and merchant alike tended in the direction not so much of labour-saving machinery as of economizing on resources and fixed capital. *Huge but nearly static markets created no bottlenecks in the production system that might have prompted creativity. . . . This situation may be described as a "high-level equilibrium trap."* . . . It is probably a sufficient explanation of the retardation of technological advance [Elvin, 1973: 314-315, emphasis added].

Note that this is not solely a technological argument at all. The entire passage, and particularly the parts to which I have added emphasis, imply a theory of markets, of entrepreneurship, of innovation, and of investment demand, all of which inevitably involve socioeconomic institutions, cultural factors, and the like. Nor does the argument require the elimination of the surplus, as Lippit assumes along with various adopters of the "trap" paradigm; in fact, the surplus can be very large ("huge but nearly static markets"), as long as it is tending to decline over time so as to rob markets of buoyancy and eliminate incentives to innovate. Unfortunately, the apparent historical constancy of agricultural output per capita deprives us of direct evidence of falling surplus, as Lippit points out. Elvin later withdrew somewhat from the "trap" formulation, especially with regard to hydraulic technology for which "there *were* better methods that did not involve science-based inputs" (Elvin, 1975: 86), and that would have been of great use in agriculture and mining. He explained the observed constancy of agricultural output per capita in terms of a rate of technological advance just sufficient to forestall diminishing returns due to population growth, and "by a process of elimination" ascribed the failure to innovate further to "cultural factors" (p. 86). This position certainly throws doubt upon the "sophisticated" version of the high-level equilibrium trap theory. Nevertheless, one wishes that economists had used the "trap" in the manner Feuerwerker now urges, namely, as "one useful intermediate tool with which to understand precisely *how* the class and social structure of Qing China actually functioned at particular times and places to obstruct the passage from premodern to modern growth"—rather than concentrating exclusively on its playful diagrammatic attributes and technological features.

LIPPIT ON THE NONDEVELOPMENT OF CHINA

Not being a historian of China, I have limited my comments largely to issues of theory and methodology. This constraint is even more of a handicap when it comes to discussing Lippit's own reasons for China's retarded development from Song times to the Republic. Lippit argues that China's failure to undergo economic modernization in the late imperial period was due essentially to the *total absence* of distinct elements within the elite favoring modernization, i.e., to the monolithic hegemony of a gentry-merchant-bureaucratic class, divided at most into upper and lower strata but not horizontally by class and economic interest. This view would seem to differ from that of Balazs chiefly in that the latter saw at least a potential differentiation between merchant and scholar-official interests, despite the absolute weakness of the merchants as a separate entity, whereas Lippit sees none at all. One wonders how significant this difference is.

As of the early nineteenth century this snapshot of Chinese social structure, in either the Balazs or the Lippit variant, seems generally accurate, and it makes clear against what odds an indigenous Chinese capitalism would have had to contend in the absence of intervention by the dynamically industrializing West. In explaining China's retarded development, Lippit is right to put great emphasis on the nature of the class structure in the late imperial period.

The way in which the characters in the snapshot assumed their positions is not at all clear, however. Feuerwerker is correct in pointing out that Lippit's explanation is itself unexplained. Indeed, in so far as a historical *process* is alluded to, it is highly ambiguous. At one point, Lippit warns against understanding the process as one of cooptation of the merchant class by the elite (since there was no separate such class to coopt). Yet, at another, he sees the elite as "over the centuries . . . incorporating within itself all of the separate groups that lived off the surplus." This is puzzling; is it meant to imply that no such "group" ever succeeded in developing into a distinct "class" before being incorporated and having the distinctions eradicated? Apparently not, since elsewhere still he talks of meaningful distinctions between officials and merchants "*as separate classes* disappear[ing]," and his treatment of late Tang and Song China explicitly includes a powerful and dynamic merchant class, improving landlords and an urban bourgeoisie. Also, early Qing times were marked by the rise of great merchants. Why then did all this not give rise to the development of a capitalist mode of production? Lippit, citing Dobb, handles this problem by drawing a parallel between the essentially conservative role of the mercantile bourgeoisie in Europe by the early seventeenth century, and that of its contemporary Chinese counterpart. In the former case, the dynamic and revolutionary role was left to be played by a class of independent capitalist producers, but in Chinese society "there was simply no space" for such a class. To illustrate the last point, however, Lippit jumps directly to 1949 figures on the insignificance of capital owned by the "national bourgeoisie." It is clear from all this that the actual processes by which formerly powerful merchant, progressive landlord and urban bourgeois classes came to be subordinated to the gentry-scholar-official elite remain to be elucidated.

After the middle of the nineteenth century, however, the situation changes under the impact of the Western presence. "The most striking social development of the period between 1872 and 1885 was the emergence of a bourgeoisie. Its nucleus was the officials, compradors, merchants, gentry, and landowners with a financial interest in modern enterprises" (Chesneaux et al., 1976: 237). This group was tied economically, socially and politically both to the traditional elite and to the foreigners. But it did develop interests of its own, particularly after the 1880s, when the *guandu shangban* system lost its grip on finance and industry and the younger generation of compradores began breaking away from both foreign and official ties to establish private enterprises of their own (Hao, 1970: 151; Chesneaux et al, 1976: 303-304). By the beginning of the twentieth century, these groups, organized around local chambers of commerce, had succeeded in achieving "a considerable degree of autonomy" from official control in the major treaty ports, and had developed a considerable class awareness (Bergère, 1968: 241, passim). The modern intellectuals, politicians, and new-style military officers mentioned by Feuerwerker were to some extent manifestations of this class, and to some extent utilized the ideology which it somewhat precociously disseminated.

This "bourgeoisie" remained weak, dependent, and of uncertain class allegiance. It was never in a position to bring about revolutionary change, and certainly did not do so in 1911. Yet it was present in the new and incredibly complex conditions of early twentieth century China, its ideological role was quite significant, and all of this should not be ignored. During World War I, when the foreign presence temporarily receded, Chinese industrial production leaped forward at exceptionally high rates, well above the long-term average (Chang, 1969: 71-73). Can we really be certain that, given several decades of respite from foreign pressures at the right point in time, such industrialization would not have created the necessary critical mass for the self-confident assertion of bourgeois interests and values? Improbable perhaps, but worth the kind of speculation that would be prematurely ended by taking too simple a view of China's class structure.

NOTES

1. These characteristics pertain to "dependence" chiefly as this concept is applied to nineteenth and early twentieth century conditions. In more recent years, with manufacturing industries growing rapidly in many less developed countries, "dependence" is seen as acquiring new forms (see, e.g., Dos Santos, 1973).

2. However, the argument as stated ("even in the 1930s imports [excluding textiles] potentially competitive with handicraft products amounted to less than 0.5% of gross domestic product [GDP], while domestic handicraft output was more than 10% of GDP") is somewhat misleading. First, imports were substantially lower in the 1930s than in some earlier years (Feuerwerker, 1968: 68), when they may have been as high as 7% of GDP. Second, handicrafts contributed about 7½% of GDP in 1933 (Liu and Yeh, 1965: 66), i.e., about the same order of magnitude as imports a decade earlier. Third, textiles declined to negligible proportions of total imports in the 1930s, but in 1920, for example, they constituted one-third of imports by value (Feuerwerker, 1968: 72). Thus, using Perkins' estimate that roughly half of imports could be considered potentially competitive with domestic handicrafts, total imports in such a position *could* have amounted to 3-4% of GDP in the first third of the twentiety century, or half the size of handicraft production.

3. The economics of this problem are elucidated in Sen (1966).

4. For example, if the extra irksomeness to the peasant of the last unit of labor performed is twice as great as the usefulness to him of the last unit of income—so that the right side of the equation has the value 2—then in equilibrium the last unit of labor must have produced just two units of income (MPL = 2) to have made the labor worthwhile. The conditions for an equilibrium are that MDL be constant or rising with labor exertions, MUY be constant or falling as income rises, and MPL be falling as labor input rises.

5. I take this occasion to acknowledge my own responsibility in this regard for having generated estimates of surplus shares of NDP to one decimal place (Riskin, 1975).

REFERENCES

BERGERE, MARIE-CLAIRE (1968) "The role of the bourgeoisie," in Mary C. Wright (ed.) China in Revolution: The First Phase, 1900-1913. New Haven and London: Yale Univ. Press.

CHANG, JOHN R. (1969) Industrial Development in Pre-Communist China. Chicago: Aldine.

CHAO, KANG (1970) Agricultural Production in Communist China, 1949-1965. Madison: Univ. of Wisconsin Press.

CHESNEAUX, JEAN, MARIANNE BASTID, and MARIE-CLAIRE BERGERE (1976) China from the Opium Wars to the 1911 Revolution. New York: Pantheon.

DERNBERGER, R. F. (1975) "The role of the foreigner in China's economic development," in D. H. Perkins (ed.) China's Modern Economy in Historical Perspective. Stanford: Stanford Univ. Press.

DOS SANTOS, T. (1973) "The structure of dependence," in Charles K. Wilber (ed.) The Political Economy of Development and Underdevelopment. New York: Random House.

ELVIN, MARK (1975) "Skills and resources in late traditional China," in D. H. Perkins (ed.) China's Modern Economy in Historical Perspective. Stanford: Stanford Univ. Press.

——— (1973) The Pattern of the Chinese Past. Stanford: Stanford Univ. Press.

ESHERICK, J. (1972) "Harvard on China: the apologetics of imperialism." Bull. of Concerned Asian Scholars 4, 4 (December).

FEUERWERKER, ALBERT (1976) The Foreign Establishment in China in the Early Twentieth Century. Ann Arbor: Center for Chinese Studies of the University of Michigan.

——— (1969) The Chinese Economy, ca. 1870-1911. Ann Arbor: Center of Chinese Studies of the University of Michigan.

——— (1968) The Chinese Economy, 1912-1949. Ann Arbor: Center for Chinese Studies of the University of Michigan.

GRIFFIN, KEITH (1974) The Political Economy of Agrarian Change. Cambridge, MA: Harvard Univ. Press.

HAO, YEN-P'ING (1970) The Compradore in Nineteenth Century China. Cambridge, MA: Harvard Univ. Press.

LIPPIT, VICTOR D. (1974) Land Reform and Economic Development in China. White Plains, New York: International Arts & Sciences Press (now M. E. Sharpe).

LIU, T. C. and K. C. YEH (1965) The Economy of the Chinese Mainland. Princeton: Princeton Univ. Press.

MOULDER, FRANCES (1977) Japan, China and the Modern World Economy. Cambridge: Cambridge Univ. Press.

MURPHEY, RHOADS (1970) The Treaty Ports and China's Modernization: What Went Wrong? Ann Arbor: Center for Chinese Studies of the University of Michigan.

NAKAMURA, JAMES I. (1966) Agricultural Production and the Economic Development of Japan, 1873-1922. Princeton: Princeton Univ. Press.

OHKAWA, KAZUSHI and HENRY ROSOVSKY (1973) Japanese Economic Growth. Stanford: Stanford Univ. Press.

PERKINS, D. H. (1975) "Growth and changing structure of China's twentieth-century economy," in D. H. Perkins (ed.) China's Modern Economy in Historical Perspective. Stanford: Stanford Univ. Press.

——— (1969) Agricultural Development in China, 1368-1968. Chicago: Aldine.

RISKIN, C. (1975) "Surplus and stagnation in modern China," in D. H. Perkins (ed.) China's Modern Economy in Historical Perspective. Stanford: Stanford Univ. Press.

SCHULTZ, THEODORE (1964) Transforming Traditional Agriculture. New Haven: Yale Univ. Press.

SEN, A. (1966) "Peasants and dualism with or without surplus labour." J. Pol. Economy 74.

Carl Riskin is Associate Professor of Economics at Queens College, City University of New York and Research Associate of the East Asian Institute, Columbia University. He is author of articles on wages and work incentives in China and on the role of small industry in Chinese development.

The Development of Underdevelopment in China

An Afterword

VICTOR D. LIPPIT
University of California, Riverside

When I submitted my article on "The Development of Under-development in China" to *Modern China*, I welcomed its use as the basis for a symposium, for I believed the historical and theoretical issues involved to be of such importance and complexity that only the clash of contending perspectives could serve to reveal them fully. For the most part, I believe that the symposium which resulted (*Modern China*, Vol. 4 No. 3, July 1978) served this purpose well. It seems to me, however, that a number of important ambiguities remain to be cleared up, and it is to pursue this purpose that I would like to present this research note.

In "The Development of Underdevelopment in China," I argued that underdevelopment in nineteenth- and twentieth-century China could not simply have meant "not yet developed," because historically, in the Song period (960-1279) for example, China was incontestably the most advanced civilization in the world. Thus, modern underdevelopment could have emerged only as the result of a historical process, the development of underdevelopment. After an admittedly cursory look at some of the important changes between the Song and modern periods,

I went on to examine some of the principal theses in the literature to see what light they could shed on the process of the development of underdevelopment in China. Some of these were sorely lacking and others provided valuable insights, but none could provide a satisfactory account of the process as a whole; so I felt it necessary to proffer my own explanation.

At the core of my explanation of the development of underdevelopment in China is the thesis that this historical process must be accounted for primarily by domestic factors rather than the thrust of colonialism and imperialism, and further, that the class structure and uses of the surplus (the share of national income above subsistence needs) were the key domestic factors. I by no means intended to belittle the pernicious impact of Western colonialism and imperialism, but merely to assert the primacy of class structure and use of the surplus, which on the one hand contributed directly to underdevelopment, and on the other formed the structure with which the exogenous factors had to interact before their force was brought to bear on Chinese society. The assertion that domestic factors were primary, it seems to me, is borne out by the fact that underdevelopment appeared prior to the time that the impact of Western imperialism became significant, and also by the fact that even when this impact became significant, it could not in itself account for the underdevelopment which Chinese society continued to manifest.

In my analysis of class structure, I placed emphasis on the increasingly monolithic character of the elite class. Conflicts between landlord and capitalist, aristocrat and bourgeois, or rentier and entrepreneur, conflicts that did so much to propel development in the West, were largely absent in China, where all of the beneficiaries of the surplus produced by peasants and workers came to constitute a single class whose objective interest could not be reconciled with economic development. This elite class, China's gentry, had two distinct strata; an upper stratum composed of high officials, big businessmen, and big landowners, and a local stratum dominating village life.[1]

Although at both levels the gentry did carry out the administrative functions necessary to keep Chinese society going, they were for the most part rentiers and parasites with minimal productive contributions, deriving their income from corruption, privilege, and monopoly. By the late imperial period, the landlords took no part in agricultural improvement, and the merchants, who obtained monopoly rights by bribing responsible officials on an exorbitant scale, typically remained aloof from the actual processes of production. As a consequence of these production relations, innovation languished and influence rather than investment was the key to success. The surplus that was generated, therefore, went into luxury consumption, expenditures on the instruments of force necessary to maintain gentry rule, and so forth; it found a variety of uses, but productive investment was not typically among these.

Although various objections to my argument were raised by the respondents, none was able to controvert my central thesis that ascribes the development of underdevelopment in China to domestic rather than exogenous forces. Even Professor Feuerwerker (1978) seems in basic agreement, despite his outrage over the violation of the virginity of "real" economic history as a discipline, which he seems to have found in my failure to provide still one more account of "output and its sectoral origin," demographic change, "the quantity and circulation of money," and so forth. In dismissing the development of underdevelopment as a "trendy notion," however, Professor Feuerwerker (1978: 332) has obscured the significance of the finding that domestic class forces have primary responsibility for bringing about the development of underdevelopment in China, a point that requires clarification.

Economic development emerged as a distinct discipline in Western social science largely in the postwar period. It appeared as both a natural outcome of the demands of the underdeveloped countries that accompanied the end of the colonial era and their emergence as independent states, and the start of the Cold War, which suddenly made the development of the Third World a pressing matter for the advanced countries. The rapid growth of the Soviet economy, beginning in 1928 with the forced industrialization ushered in by the five-year plans, had many evident attractions as a model of development for the Third World, and the search for alternatives inevitably found a place near the top of the intellectual agenda in the West. This search emerged, at the same time, in the context of the widespread acceptance of Keynesian economic analysis, which shifted attention from the behavior of atomistic individuals to that of national economies and macroeconomic policy, and the Harrod-Domar model of economic growth, which focused on savings and investment as the strategic variables in economic growth.

Out of this background emerged the mainstream of economic development analysis, based on a paradigm which treats increased capital formation and the technological progress accompanying it as the most important factors in development. Trade and aid are, in this view, engines of development, increasing the resources available for investment and facilitating the international transmission of technology from more-developed to less-developed countries, in addition to providing the benefits associated with the principle of comparative advantage. Contact with the more-developed countries, therefore, is seen in the orthodox paradigm as promoting development. Underdevelopment, accordingly, is treated as meaning "not yet developed," and the process of development is understood as merely one of historical latecomers treading the same path the advanced countries once did.

This orthodox conception of underdevelopment is sorely deficient in a number of respects, for in effectively denying the underdeveloped countries a history, it effaces the major role the advanced countries have played in creating and sustaining underdevelopment. Indeed, in carrying out the plunder of resources and the economic transformations toward plantation agriculture that served their own development, the advanced countries have been a primary force in the creation of underdevelopment. It is thanks to the pathbreaking work of Andre Gunder Frank more than anyone else, and to his historical research on the development of underdevelopment in Latin America, that we can see so clearly that underdevelopment emerges as the result of a historical process and that this process has intertwined the progress of some parts of the world with a form of retrogression in other parts. A major empirical-historical question that remains, however, is whether the preeminent role imperialism-colonialism has played in creating underdevelopment in some parts of the world is characteristic of the underdevelopment process everywhere.

A still more significant question concerns the role of the domestic class structure and the relations of production in generating and sustaining underdevelopment. Professor Frank's formulations tend to ascribe an almost determining role to the exogenous forces, as though the capitalist world system encountered a tabula rasa in the areas upon which it encroached and created from scratch a social and class structure accommodated to its own needs. The fact that by far the greater share of the surplus generated in underdeveloped countries is disposed of domestically, however, should alert us to the danger of neglecting endogenous forces. My own position is that underdevelopment emerges as a historical process through the interaction of domestic class structure and the international impact of colonialism and imperialism, and that in this interaction either the domestic forces or the foreign ones may be primary in particular cases. Although Professor Griffin (1968: 354) attributes a somewhat different position to me, I believe I am substantially in complete agreement with him in this regard. As far as the Chinese case is concerned, I believe that my study points both to the mutual interaction and to the primacy of internal forces. Although Professor Riskin (1968: 360) chooses to define the concept of the development of underdevelopment in the way Professor Frank has used it, as one implying external dependence and victimization by imperialism in general, I see no objection to treating the development of underdevelopment as a historical process involving domestic as well as external causes.

The most important criticism to emerge in the symposium is Professor Frank's observation, seconded by Professor Riskin, that I have not adequately demonstrated the way in which underdevelopment emerged (Frank, 1978: 343-344). I believe this to be a fair criticism. In showing an advanced society in the thirteenth century, an underdeveloped one in the nineteenth century, and suggesting that the transition from one to the other unequivocally implies the development of underdevelopment as a historical process, my argument emerges more as a kind of comparative statics than as an elucidation of historical dynamics. Although as a development economist rather than a historian I believe I lack the qualifications to clarify these dynamics, I would hope that the theses I suggest will provide a useful framework for doing so. That this is indeed possible is suggested by Professor Feuerwerker's (1978: 333) reference to a "by now quite immense literature in Chinese, Japanese and Western languages which might either support or contradict" my argument. Although he says nothing about its content, I would hope that scholars more knowledgeable in this area of Chinese history than either of us can contribute to the discussion.

I believe it is important in this context to reassert the importance of appropriate theoretical perspectives in empirical or historical studies. It is not, as Professor Feuerwerker would have us believe, simply a matter of getting on with the business of studying "real" economic history by throwing into the pot all available theoretical perspectives, for theory really does shape what is studied, how it is approached, and what conclusions are reached. The incorrect theories concerning China's underdevelopment that have remained until now largely unchallenged—such as the idea that China was "not yet developed" or that its underdevelopment reflected a taste for high culture rather than material gain—have contributed to massive misunderstandings of Chinese history, while causing really fundamental issues to remain uninvestigated and difficult even to perceive.

Thus the major conclusion to which Professor Elvin's (1973: 315) concept of the "high-level equilibrium trap" leads him is: "It was the historic contribution of the modern West to ease and then break the high-level equilibrium trap in China." This positive assessment of imperialism and its impact derives directly from the theory itself, and I believe it is improper for Professors

Feuerwerker (1978: 338) and Riskin (1978: 372) to continue to advocate the use of such a demonstrably incorrect theory (Lippit, 1978: 287-294) on the grounds that it remains "one useful intermediate tool with which to understand precisely *how* the class and social structure of Qing China actually functioned at particular times and places to obstruct the passage from pre-modern to modern growth." Since the "trap" is incorrect theoretically, and specifically draws attention away from the social and class structure of Qing China, it is not possible to use it in the way Professors Riskin and Feuerwerker urge. This would appear to be one more example of the widespread confusion in Western social science between "tools" and theory, the erroneous belief that such tools or theory can be value-free, and the belief that truth can be revealed by an agnostic amalgam of bits and pieces of all available theories brought to bear on an endless array of "facts."

None of the responses by the symposium participants has undercut my central theses that underdevelopment in China emerged as a historical process, that endogenous factors were primarily responsible, and that among these the class structure together with the relations of production and surplus use were **most important**. While these theses obviously need further substantiation, studies which proceed along these lines can, I submit, reveal much about the development of underdevelopment in China and open up new perspectives in the study of Chinese history.

I would also hope that my exploration of the Chinese case can contribute to the study of the development of underdevelopment in Third World countries generally. In the last analysis, I fully subscribe to Professor Griffin's view (1978: 354) that "internal and external forces, in a process of mutual causation, interact on each other to produce underdevelopment," and that "there is no reason in principle why it should be impossible to detect primary causal responsibility for the process of underdevelopment or to attribute relative importance to internal and external elements." By showing that internal factors were more important in the Chinese case and by focusing on the role of class structure among these factors, I would hope that some tendency in the literature of economic development to exaggerate the force of exogenous influences and neglect the role of indigenous class structures in the creation and perpetuation of underdevelopment will be corrected, and that more balanced assessments of their mutual interaction and differing relative importance from country to country will be recognized.

NOTE

1. Although a tendency toward increasing class differentiation became evident in the second half of the nineteenth century, this was only after Chinese underdevelopment had already been established. Thus this tendency made only marginal inroads on the power of the gentry class before the twentieth century.

REFERENCES

ELVIN, MARK (1978) "Comment." Modern China 4, 3: 329-330.
——— (1973) The Pattern of the Chinese Past. Stanford, CA: Stanford Univ. Press.
FEUERWERKER, A. (1978) "A white horse may or may not be a horse, but megahistory is not economic history." Modern China 4, 3: 331-339.
FRANK, A. G. (1978) "Development of underdevelopment or underdevelopment of development in China." Modern China 4, 3: 341-350.
GRIFFIN, K. (1978) "The roots of underdevelopment: reflections on the Chinese experience." Modern China 4, 3: 351-357.
LIPPIT, V. (1978) "The development of underdevelopment in China." Modern China 4, 3: 251-328.
RISKIN, C. (1978) "The symposium papers: discussion and comments." Modern China 4, 3: 359-376.

Victor D. Lippit is Associate Professor of Economics at the University of California, Riverside. He is the author of Land Reform and Economic Development in China: A Study of Institutional Change and Development Finance. *He is currently working on a new book,* The Economic Development of China, *to be published by M. E. Sharpe.*